MAKING SPACE

MAKING SPACE

How to Decorate and Renovate to Get the Space You Need from the Space You Have

By Sally Clark & Lois Perschetz

Clarkson N. Potter, Inc./Publishers
DISTRIBUTED BY CROWN PUBLISHERS, INC.
NEW YORK

To Bob Bayne and Arthur Perschetz
for their encouragement, support,
and unfailing enthusiasm

Copyright © 1983 by Sally Clark and Lois Perschetz
Grateful acknowledgment is made for permission to reprint the following photographs: pages 8, 33 (bottom), 42–43, 56, 64, 66–69, 72–73, 92, 104, 112–13, 145, 165 (right), 168, 169 (bottom left and right), 170, 174–75, 180 (top center), 181, 184, 187, 193–218

Published by Clarkson N. Potter, Inc., One Park Avenue, New York, New York 10016, and simultaneously in Canada by General Publishing Company Limited

Manufactured in Italy

Library of Congress Cataloging in Publication Data

Clark, Sally.
　　Making space.

　　Includes index.
　　1. Space (Architecture)　　2. Interior architecture.
3. Buildings—Remodeling for other use.　　4. Room layout
(Dwellings).　　5. Personal space.　　I. Perschetz, Lois.
II. Title.
NA2765.C45　　1983　　　　728'.028'6　　　　83–9505
ISBN: 0-517-54716-3

10 9 8 7 6 5 4 3 2 1

First Edition

ACKNOWLEDGMENTS

The making of this book was a wonderful adventure that led us to many helpful people. We'd like to thank everyone who took the time to give us encouragement, provide insights, and direct us to the marvelous locations in the pages that follow.

We'd especially like to give thanks to:

All the designers and architects who allowed us to photograph their work, and the homeowners who so kindly let us into their homes with our cameras.

The photographers we worked with—James Levin, Peter Loppacher, Ralph Bogertman, and Norman McGrath. We thank them for their enthusiasm about the project and the fine photography that contributes so much to this book.

The manufacturers who were so cooperative in supplying the information and photographs for the product section.

Our agents, Gayle Benderoff and Deborah Geltman, who realized that "making space" is a problem everyone relates to.

All the people at Clarkson N. Potter who guided this book through its production with such care and interest—Nancy Novogrod, our editor; Michael Fragnito, director of operations; and Gael Dillon, who supervised the art direction.

Hermann Strohbach, who designed the book and made a handsome volume out of the hundreds of slides and countless lines of copy we gave him.

Leslie Gill for drawing the floor plans that clarify the space solutions in Part Two and Part Three.

We'd also like to thank the helpful people who made particular photography sessions go so smoothly. They are: Tom Marshall of Marshall & Company for a spectacular last-minute flower arrangement; Diantha Nype and the Show House committee for so graciously allowing us to photograph rooms at the 1982 Kips Bay Boys' Club Decorator Show House; Michael Malcé of Kelter-Malcé for providing a beautiful blue-and-white quilt when we needed it in a hurry; Edward Munves, Jr., of James Robinson for supplying the dazzling flatware that was the finishing touch; Bob Michielutti of Pierre Deux for loaning us wonderful accessories with such efficient speed; Kitty Sorrell, who sent a handsome array of Garrett Wade tools posthaste; Flo Wilson at Knoll, who lent us the perfect white tables when we called; Penny Sikalis at Gear Design for the sheets and accessories; Ken Nelson for providing the Closet Maid shelving that transformed an insignificant space into a terrific one, and the people at Closet King for installing it; Harriet Schoenthal, who found us a much-needed Syroco folding shelf; and Black & Decker, whose inch-wide step stool gave us an extra boost in *Making Space*.

There are also some special people we've met along the way in our publishing careers to whom we'd like to give a nod of thanks for their influence and for their encouragement—JoAnn Barwick, Betty Boote, Michael Coady, John Fairchild, Gordon Firth, Etta Froio, Samuel Pennington, and June Weir.

CONTENTS

Space is becoming a luxury. For most Americans, this is a startling realization. The idea of an ever-expanding horizon is an essential part of our heritage. The vast lands that unfolded forever were the lure that attracted many of our ancestors. And as land became too settled or overfarmed, they could simply push west, where open land awaited for farming, home-building, and city-making.

In more recent memory, the booming development of the suburbs following World War II was a latter-day version of American expansion. The dotting of the suburban landscape with look-alike structures from builders' plan books, all in neatly measured lots with family rooms, multiple bedrooms, separate dining rooms, and attached garages, signaled America's postwar prosperity. It seemed to hold the promise that homeownership would be possible for every middle-class American, then and forever.

But today, a recessionary economy, spiraling inflation, high energy costs, and high mortgages have severely altered that expectation for many young families. In this economy the housing picture has changed dramatically. We are caught in a space squeeze that touches all types of housing—in cities and suburbs, in rentals and private homes, in houses and apartments.

With building costs up, the size of houses being constructed is shrinking substantially. The median size of new homes built in 1978 was 1,655 square feet. In 1981, the figure was down to 1,550 square feet. By 1985, some experts predict, the average new house will have shrunk to 1,200 square feet.

Space in these new houses is at a premium. Not only are the rooms smaller than in the typical builder house of 20 years ago, but some rooms have been eliminated completely. Formal dining rooms, for example, have vanished; now the living room is expected to do double duty as family dining space.

Gone, too, is the fourth bedroom that had become standard in typical suburban homes of the 1960s, and, in many instances today, there is not even a third bedroom. Also eliminated are gracious entry foyers and the hallways separating the "public" living areas from the family sleeping quarters. More and more in these houses, the same room has to serve many functions. Or, to put it another way, the same place has to be dealt with inventively to accommodate many activities.

ONE

BREAKING OUT OF THE SPACE BIND

Faced with the smaller size of today's new homes—and fazed by higher mortgage rates—families who own houses are often opting to renovate rather than move. In 1980, Americans spent an estimated $54 billion on remodeling, outstripping the sum spent on new-home construction.

Garages are being turned into living rooms, once-cramped kitchens expanded into airy kitchen-family rooms, and master bedroom/bath wings added that rival the local health club in spa-like amenities. Such renovations are not inexpensive, but they are far less costly than gaining the same space in a new home, and the homeowners feel they are getting more for their investments.

Remodeling has also become a way of life for many city apartment dwellers, and not just for those who own their homes. In New York City, for example, where rents of new apartments have skyrocketed, tenants paying moderate sums for the apartments they have are putting money into space-making design instead of moving to bigger, more expensive quarters. These design treatments can run into major expenditures, but higher rents and the cost of moving make it easy to rationalize the expense.

So does the stingy size of most of the new apartments being constructed. For as with new homes, developers of new apartment buildings are squeezing space where they can. This usually means ceilings no higher than 9 feet, kitchens as tiny as ship's galleys, and minimum storage space.

The shortage of apartment space in cities around the country has added fire to the preservationist movement and encouraged the transformation of more and more old nonresidential buildings into new apartment complexes. Even vintage commercial buildings of no great architectural beauty—factories, garages, and hotels—are being recycled.

Developers' efforts to make every inch count in these reconstituted buildings often produce oddly configured spaces. Living rooms shaped like bowling alleys and bedrooms with cramped floor space underfoot and soaring ceilings overhead challenge even the most inventive interior designer, not to mention the untrained homeowner.

The economy is not the only factor triggering changes in housing. Enormous social changes are taking place that are dramatically altering the kinds of housing Americans need. Statistics, in fact, indicate that for many people, smaller homes are actually going to be more desirable in the future.

According to the 1980 census, the number of people per household declined from 3.14 in 1970 to 2.76 in 1980. Smaller houses with fewer bedrooms, baths, and family spaces would seem to make sense.

There are other factors to consider as well. The number of two-income couples is on the upswing, meaning there is no one at home to care for the house. Some of these couples have opted out of parenthood entirely; for others, having a family may mean raising only one child. The ideal home for many of these people, especially to those without children, is a home that can be left worry-free during the trips in which the couple is apt to indulge.

The growing number of single-parent households (one out of five children lives with only one parent) is another factor contributing to the shrinking average household size. The large house that well served a two-parent family in marriage often becomes a white elephant in divorce. More manageable and economical space is wanted instead.

Statistics also tell us that more people live alone today than ever before. The divorced, separated, widowed, and never-married are all part of this group. So are the growing number of young people who choose to remain single longer than their parents did, delaying marriage and child-rearing until they are well established in a career.

Housing requirements for all these singles may best be met by compact space, easily maintained space—and perhaps by the spaces designed into nontraditional living quarters.

The building industry has begun to answer the housing needs of a changing population with innovative alternatives. Attached homes, which the National Association of Home Builders estimates accounted for 20 percent of all new construction in 1982, are one of the best choices for people who want the feeling of a house with the easy maintenance of an apartment.

The average two-bedroom unit built in 1982 added up to a truly compact 930 square feet, with each bedroom measuring 11 by 12 feet. The single working adult, the two-income couple, and the single parent with a child can all find convenience here: no lawn to mow, fewer extra rooms to clean and heat.

The shared house is another solution recently developed by the home-building industry as the demand for alternative types of housing grows.

Pioneered in western and Sunbelt cities such as

Angeles, Dallas, Miami, and Orlando, the shared house is intended for two or more unrelated buyers, who can share purchase and upkeep costs while each enjoys the emotional benefits of having his or her own home. Shared houses generally feature central common spaces such as living rooms and kitchens, with separate wings housing master bedroom/bathroom suites to which each owner can retreat for privacy.

Who buys tandem houses? Single adults who find them a perfect financial solution for homeownership; a divorced parent with child who joins forces

HOW TO WORK WITH AN INTERIOR DESIGNER

The preliminaries. People hire interior designers for a variety of reasons. Some people realize that they don't have the skill or imagination to handle the job. Others don't have the time. And still others want an image—"drop-dead" chic, slick contemporary, or "instant-heritage" traditional. They hire a designer known for a particular look who can help them achieve the image they want.

A good interior designer is an interpreter who translates your tastes and needs into an environment that is comfortable, functional, and pleasing to look at.

There are many ways to find an interior designer. Get in touch with local professional organizations, or ask friends for recommendations. Visit the designer showcase houses that are held as charity events in cities and suburbs throughout the country. Decorating magazines are also a good source.

Interview several designers before hiring one. Be clear about your budget and about what you hope to accomplish with the design project. Be sure to see photographs of work the designer has recently completed, which will attest to whether his work looks fresh.

In the initial interview the designer should ask questions about the scope of the job, your space and storage needs, and how the rooms you are planning to redo should function for the life you lead.

Before proceeding with the designer whose work and approach appeals to you, you might ask to visit some actual jobs he or she has just completed. Seeing the rooms will give you insights that are sometimes difficult to derive from photographs. Does the traffic pattern work? Is the room comfortable to be in? Is there enough seating? Are there enough tables and surfaces to rest a glass on, display a collection, and keep much-used items near at hand? Is the lighting well positioned? Is the scale of the furnishings appropriate and harmonious? Is the overall design successful?

The specifics. Shortly after agreeing to work with you, the designer will probably draw up a contract. Although contracts differ from one designer to another, the agreement typically outlines the extent of the job and the terms of payment. Later on you will get estimates detailing particular furniture, fabrics, and items to be included.

Although there is no set system of fees in the interior-design business, most designers charge clients in one of several ways, or in combination:

- By the hour: Some designers charge by the hour when the job is small. Others charge by the hour regardless of the scope of the job.
- Flat fee: Usually arrived at based on the extent of the work and the amount of time the designer gauges it will take to complete the job.
- Percentage: Some designers charge a percentage of what the total job—concept, labor, and materials—will cost, usually 20 to 25 percent, as their design fee.
- Mark-up: Say the designer sells you a sofa that is purchased from a professional "to-the-trade" source. The mark-up between the price the designer pays and the price to you, usually 30 to 40 percent, represents the profit he or she makes on the transaction.

Read the contract and all estimates carefully. Never give the go-ahead until you are absolutely clear on the work that will be done. If you don't understand something, ask.

If an item you thought you were getting isn't mentioned, query it. Don't assume that the sofa will be upholstered with a skirt, or the pillows will have Turkish corners, just because you had envisioned it. Double-check everything.

By the same token, have as clear an idea as possible of what the final job will look like. If you can't grasp the floor plans and swatches the designer presents, ask to have a rendering, or drawing, done of the projected room. There

will probably be an extra fee for the rendering, but it's worth it if you're having trouble imagining how the room will eventually look.

You may find the contractor, or the designer may do it, if major renovation is involved. Some designers do have particular contractors they prefer working with and consider supervision of construction work part of their design job.

It is the designer's responsibility to come up with a plan that fits your budget. If the estimates for the job come in higher than the original budget, it's up to the designer to rework the design so that it stays in line with the amount you originally intended to spend.

Your role. Realize that the interior designer is one of the last of the custom professionals. The dressmaker, milliner, and bootmaker have all vanished. But the interior designer continues to produce custom, one-of-a-kind design work. Custom work takes time.

You should also be aware that the interior designer is an intermediary. He or she relies on a fleet of other professionals—painters, upholsterers, and specialized craftsmen—to get the job done. Foul-ups do occur. The sofa may get delayed at the upholsterer's. The painter may get backed up in his work schedule. The custom-dyed fabric that was supposed to be delicate peach could arrive in bright orange. Be prepared for setbacks.

You can sit passively by and let the designer choose everything for you. But if you get engaged in the process, it will be much more exciting. Most designers welcome the client who shows an active interest as the transformation takes place. Working with the designer to select accent pieces, accessories, and antiques is the best way to become involved in the process, since it allows you to add your personality to the environment the professional is creating. And it's a sure way to be entirely satisfied with the final look of the room.

HOW TO WORK WITH A CONTRACTOR

The decision is made. The walls are to go up or down, a room revamped or added on. Who hires the contractor? You do. Although some designers prefer to use their own workmen (which will be explained in the designer's arrangements with you), in most instances you are the one directly responsible for the contractor, whom you will be hiring to implement your desires or the designer's plan.

As with any workman, the best way to find a good contractor is through satisfied customers. Ask your friends, neighbors, even the owners of stores whose interior construction you admire. Then call potential candidates to come to inspect the proposed job.

The more explicit you are about your plans, the better able he will be to bid your job accurately. Be specific about everything—the design, the quality of materials, and the particular lights, windows, doors, heaters, and so on to be included (by brand and model, if possible). Don't assume anything: If it's not on the plan or list of specifications, it won't be included—even if it's something you would consider as obvious as doorknobs. And if an item's not included, it's an "extra" you will have to pay for later in addition to your agreed-upon price.

When you interview contractors, ask if they have done this kind of job before, the names of references, what kind of insurance they carry, whether or not they guarantee their work and for how long, how they expect to be paid, when they can start the job, how long they plan for it to take, and what their price

is. Then, check references, compare bids, and make your decision.

The job begins. Be clear with the contractor about working hours. It is important for your family and the contractor to be aware of one another's schedules, and, if you live in an apartment, your building probably has restrictions about hours during which work can take place.

All construction—no matter how minor you may think it is—is messy. Don't expect a contractor to treat your home like his own. Pack away whatever you can, seal up the edges of closets with masking tape, put dropcloths on furniture, place heavy paper or old sheets on the floors where workmen will be walking.

Remember that the contractor will be bringing building materials and tools. Make sure you have a place for him to put them. And a place for him to put his waste as well. (Will he take it away, or are you responsible? Ask.)

Go over the plans again. You may have changed your mind about something; one of you may have forgotten an item already discussed. Be clear about details: Don't assume he will use white light switches and plates just because your walls are white, or that he will install doorknobs 34 inches high like the others in your house if he's used to installing them 36 inches high.

During the job, you will probably think about some changes and ask, "Can you put an extra light here?" "Can you move this outlet?" Never forget that the

contractor's classic answer is, "Sure, I can do that." What he may not tell you is that it will cost extra to have him do it. Make sure you know before he begins.

Inspect the work as often as possible. (Or, if you are paying your architect or designer to do that, make sure that he or she does.) Insist it be done the way you specified, not the way that is easier or the way he is accustomed to doing it. If a change is necessary, because either a mistake has been made or you have reconsidered the design, you want to catch it early before it is too difficult or costly to correct.

Pay the contractor as specified in your agreement or contract. Most will require an initial payment and then several more as the work progresses. If the contract calls for a payment when framing is completed, for example, pay when it is completed and not a day before. Make sure your payment schedule allows for a large enough payment at the end to ensure there's incentive for the contractor to take care of those small problems that invariably arise and to complete the job.

The job is finished. Walk through the job with the contractor, inspect it again carefully on your own, make a "punch list" of *anything* that needs completing or adjusting, whether it's a door that doesn't close properly or electrical outlet plates that need straightening. The final payment should be turned over only when *everything* is done to your satisfaction.

---

with another single parent, for financial and sometimes emotional support; and couples who buy tandem units as second homes to share with another couple for weekends and vacations.

Sharing housing of all kinds is, in fact, becoming more prevalent in the 1980s. In a tight economy, young people graduating from college are finding themselves back home with their parents because they can't afford apartments of their own. Young married couples are moving in with parents until they can save enough money to buy their own house—a situation not seen since the housing squeeze following World War II—and older parents are moving in with their grown children.

What all this means is that space has suddenly be-

come a problem for everybody. The parents who expected to have an empty nest now find themselves making room for grown offspring. But the room that served the youngster is now too cramped and outmoded for the young adult who commutes to a job every day. The question then becomes how to redesign that space to function for today's needs.

What about the single adult who's just purchased a condominium? He or she is thrilled to be a homeowner, but how to deal with the tight space of the living room? What's the best way to handle those low ceilings that suddenly became claustrophobic when the movers arrived with the furniture?

What's the solution for the family who bought a new house ten years ago and now find themselves cramped for space? If remodeling is a better investment than moving, what's the best way to do it? Do they renovate the attic to get the extra bedrooms they need? Do they remodel the garage to get that big family kitchen they've been dreaming of?

And what about the two-income couple both of whom bring work home at night? How can they carve space for two home offices out of a one-bedroom apartment and still have privacy?

And how can a young couple accommodate the newly arrived second child in a small two-bedroom house that's filled with charm but lacking in space?

THE SPACE PROBLEM: TIPS ON COPING

This book has been written in an attempt to answer these questions. Whether you live in a large house or a tiny apartment, you probably have space problems. Right off the bat, most interior-design specialists would probably tell you you aren't even using the space you have to maximum efficiency.

- How about the home office you'd love to have? Have you considered converting that unused closet in the back hall into a private work area? What about redesigning the dining room that's used only for holiday sit-down meals, so that it can do double duty as an office and study?
- And what about double-duty rooms? If you need space for exercising, have you thought of reworking the guest room to make space for your exercise equipment? If you need space for an overnight guest, have you considered redesigning the dining room with, say, banquette seating that might convert into a guest bed?
- Would double-duty furniture solve some of your space problems? A custom piece might be the answer to your particular situation, but there is also a wide range of double-duty furnishings available in stores. These include ottomans that open up to beds and coffee tables that convert to dining height.
- What about the kitchen? Have you thought of a cantilevered counter to get the space for a breakfast area? Have you considered a work island on casters that could be moved around to provide additional counter space where needed? Instead of builder cabinets that stop a few feet short of the ceiling, have you thought of floor-to-ceiling cabinets to maximize storage?
- What about the closets? Are they outfitted with double rods, which might put the space to its fullest use? Would a wire shelving system give you more storage?
- Look up. Are you really taking advantage of all the wall space clear up to the ceiling? Couldn't you put cabinets overhead to store seasonal items? Couldn't you add high shelves for books you don't need to reach every day? Couldn't you display your prized pottery up there?

The interiors shown on the following pages can be a guide to inspire space-making ideas for your own home. Some of them are the work of professional interior designers and architects; others are the creative solutions of innovative homeowners.

The range of styles in these rooms proves that making more space does not mean adhering to one particular style or concept. Although the philosophy that less is more is the guiding principle to which some people adhere in making a space work better or look larger, it is not the only concept to follow. Personal mementos, inviting art, idiosyncratic furniture, and antique pieces should also be able to find their place in a small room, if that is the way you want to live. There are many rooms in this book that prove that a small space can be made into a stylishly decorated jewel that is traditional, warm, and highly personal.

Making the limitations of your space work for you requires a sense of adventure and a willingness to engage the imagination. As with all decorating, the best rooms are those that reflect the personality, taste, and wit of the person who lives there.

Start by studying all your options. Perhaps a total renovation will get you the most efficient solution to your space problems. But you may discover that by rethinking the space you have and being more flexible in redesigning it, you can make it function beautifully for your life-style. The interiors that follow are intended as a departure point for your own space-making inventions. The imagination with which others have solved their problems should inspire you to come up with your own ways of getting the space you need out of the space you already have.

Houses are shrinking. Prices are skyrocketing. "Making do" and "making over" are words we seem to hear more often these days than "moving on." This is the reality. Big, rambling houses in which every family member has a room of his or her own, and each domestic function has a room of its own, have gone the way of giant-size luxury cars. But we can remember them with affection and, as with cars, enjoy the challenge of exploring smaller creations that are new and exciting, innovative, exceedingly efficient—and may well meet our needs far better than the old ones ever did.

How many people are there in your household? According to statistics, you may well live alone, with just a mate, or just one child. Do you really need a four- or five-bedroom house like the one you or your parents (and possibly four or five siblings) may have grown up in? Well-designed smaller housing might meet your needs far better, especially if the adults in the household are working and there is no one staying at home to care for the house.

On the other hand, do you live in a small house and find you would like a little more space than you have, whether it's a larger living room or kitchen, more bedrooms, or a private place for that grown child who went off to college four years ago and now, after graduation, finds that he/she can't afford to live on his/her own? That space might be lurking within your house, being used for storage or not at all, and ripe for renovation.

Have you always dreamed of living in a conventional house surrounded by a lush green lawn, only to find now that that style of living is not within your budget? Or not available where you want to live? Or that you would enjoy living in a space not quite so traditional?

In this section, we will show you real-life situations and real-life solutions: houses and apartments that are small by design (pages 16 through 49); how people are stretching for space by converting attics, basements, and garages into exciting, highly usable spaces (pages 50 through 63); and new-style housing so appealing it will give new meaning to the American Dream of a home of one's own (pages 64 through 81).

PETER LOPPACHER

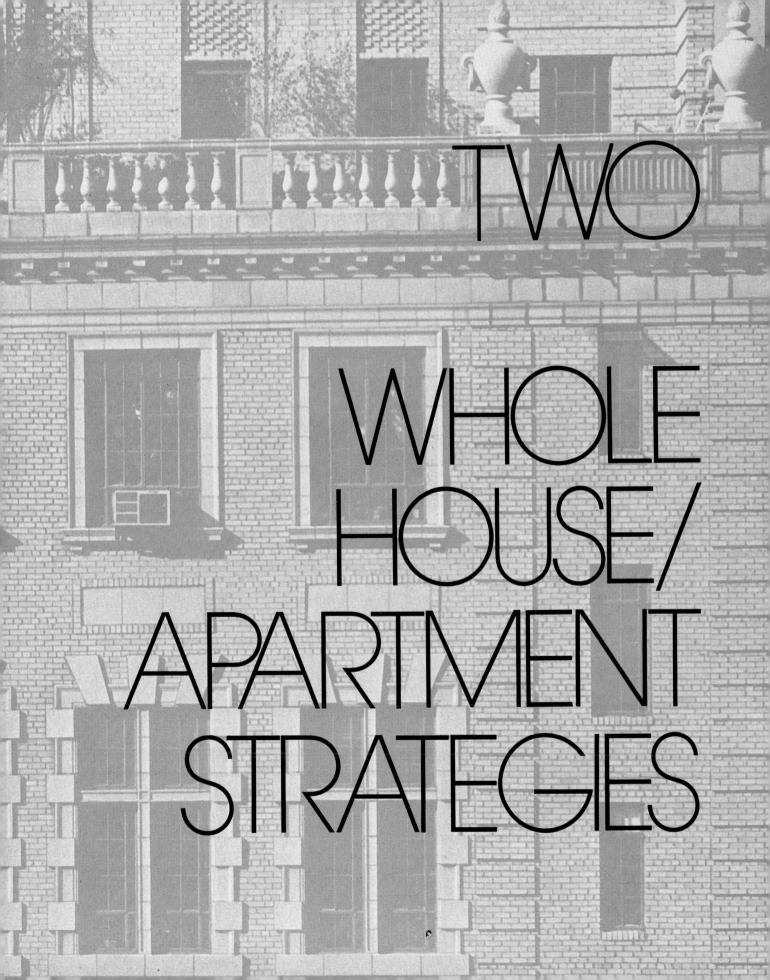

TWO
WHOLE HOUSE/ APARTMENT STRATEGIES

SMALL BY DESIGN

There is much to be said for a home that is small. Wouldn't you rather have a flawless one-carat diamond than a two-carat one that's not quite so perfect? So, too, with houses. A gem of a house brings us pleasure visually, and pleasure, too, from the satisfaction of knowing how perfectly it functions for us. As Billy Baldwin, the noted decorator who has always chosen to live in small spaces, has often been quoted as saying, "Small size doesn't have to mean small style." And that is vitally important to remember. It is just as possible to give an 8-by-10-foot box of a room great style as it is one three times that size—and, quite logically, for about one-third the cost. Don't forget that a huge house or apartment that seems like "a bargain" to buy or rent may not be quite such a bargain when you figure out how much furniture and carpet it needs. Nor may it be such a bargain when it comes to taking care of it.

There are, of course, other reasons why one would choose a small home just for the joy of it. For vacations, certainly, when swimming and skiing and tennis-playing are much more pleasurable than cleaning house or preparing elaborate dinner parties. And, similarly, when a busy family/work/social schedule makes it nice to have a home that's easy to maintain. Or just because we opt for paying less—in purchase price or rent—and saving our money for other things. There are also times when we may have outgrown the particular place in which we live, but are too emotionally attached to it or its neighborhood to move.

For all these reasons, out of choice, we select a home that is small by design—a home that challenges our ingenuity but by no means cramps our style.

Opposite: Built about 300 years ago with a later addition that gives it its present saltboxlike silhouette, this 22-by-30-foot house has survived the ever-changing needs of owners who reshaped its interior accordingly. For the present owner, however, the way to make the small house function best today was to restore it to its original plan. The entire house is shown on the following pages.

An Early Cape: America's Original Small House

This is how the most typical of American small houses, the Cape Cod, actually began: as a spare little one-story cottage with gable roof and wood-shingled exterior weathered by the salty sea air. Very straightforward and eminently functional, it usually had a one-room interior that was used for cooking, eating, sleeping, and visiting.

A very early example of a Cape Cod, the house shown here was built around 1680 in Southampton, New York, by the Hand family, whose members numbered among the original 20 settlers of eastern Long Island and which later included Captain David Hand, who fought in the Revolutionary War. As Captain Hand became more and more involved with whaling, the house was moved progressively closer to port until, after three moves, it found its present home in the village of Sag Harbor. As owners and their needs changed, the house underwent many transformations. Walls went up and down, and an addition was attached to the rear.

Today it belongs to photographer/antiques-shop owner Otto Fenn, who has restored to the house a functional style of living similar to that of the early settlers: Downstairs activities take place in a small living room and one great room used for cooking, dining, and guest sleeping quarters.

Right, opposite top and bottom: With cooking, dining, and sleeping taking place all in one room, this is a modern-day version of an early keeping room. The kitchen is so well planned in its compactness that everything, including the stove, refrigerator, and sink, is within arm's reach. Spices are on shelves tucked between the windows, and racks at the windows' tops and bottoms hold glasses. The sink counter has open shelves facing the kitchen, doors on the side facing the dining table. Since the open kitchen is visible from the entire room, Mr. Fenn grain-painted and combed the refrigerator and chose a decorative copper sink, sunk into a 3-inch cherry-wood slab. The use of cupboard beds, heavy pieces of furniture with doors or curtains to seal off the cold night air, was a Dutch tradition brought to America. The piece Mr. Fenn uses here, for overnight guests, is a freestanding French Brittany bed.

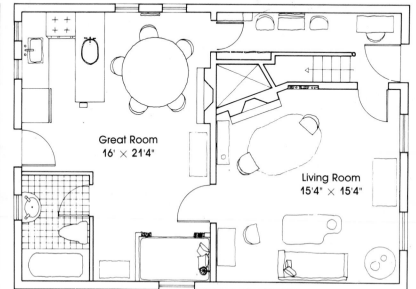

Great Room
16' × 21'4"

Living Room
15'4" × 15'4"

Above: Two small bedrooms now occupy the attic space. This one measures 7 by 7 feet, and with its book recesses and low-post bed reaching almost end to end, it has the feel of a ship's stateroom. **Left:** Decorative reminders of the house's association with the whaling industry, scrimshaw and sailors' whimsies are displayed in the living room, where a curly maple dropleaf table, seen here with its sides down, can be opened in front of the fireplace and the Windsor chairs pulled up for winter suppers. Doors to the right of the fireplace hide television and record player.

Reshaping a Traditional Floor Plan

If the home you have chosen—for whatever reason—is small and you feel limited by the space as it exists, there are three ways of dealing with it:

- Taking the limitations and decorating around them (see pages 26 through 29)
- Doing some modular building without altering the original space (pages 30 through 33)
- And, definitely the most radical and generally the most expensive, tearing down and rebuilding the interior

That was the case with this 800-square-foot apartment, which is in a somewhat staid, old masonry apartment building. When the owners bought it, it was a conventional maze of hallways and insular rooms. What they asked designer Horace Gifford to give them was interrelated, functional spaces that would be easy to maintain, plus abundant storage, which immediately cut down on the available floor space. The home that Mr. Gifford carved for them has a surprisingly unchanged layout, but it is now an exciting, free-flowing series of spaces that is full of curves and mirrored surfaces, both large and small (see plan, page 25). "Because of all the curves," he says, "there is an ambiguity as to scale—and more apparent space than there really is."

The hallway (photographed at right from the front door) immediately sets the stage. "The length of the hallway in such a tiny apartment gives you a sense of arrival, of being handled as you come in," says the designer. All walls are made of exterior stucco, an easy-to-maintain material Mr. Gifford

chose because he wanted the apartment to have the same sense of strength and permanence as the building in which it is located.

Opposite bottom left: Now the entrance hallway leads right to the kitchen, the most-used room and the focal point of the apartment. Measuring approximately 9 by 16 feet, it is about twice the size of the original kitchen. **Opposite top:** The owners, both of whom travel frequently, didn't want a great deal of living or sleeping space, or furniture. Mr. Gifford pared the living room down to a wall-to-wall banquette, two ottomans, and a system of waferlike tables that can be stacked or moved around as needed. **Opposite bottom right:** Dominating one living-room wall like a piece of minimal sculpture, a construction designed by Mr. Gifford opens to reveal a guest bed. Bedding is stored in a mirrored closet abutting the left end of the banquette.

Opposite: The dining room's success is owed as much to what you don't see as to what you do. At its simplest, the space is clean and spare, with only four chairs and a marble slab mounted on a single pedestal. Five shallow closets do the rest of the work, holding glassware, liquor, four folding Plia chairs for additional guests, even cookbooks and "office" supplies.

Left top: For entertaining, the dining room takes on drama from the mirrored closet wall and a table that pivots to a diagonal to give the room the illusion of more space.

Left center: The bedroom is just one step up, separated from the dining room by panels on pivot hinges. Closed, they give both the rooms architectural interest; open, they allow the owners to enjoy the spaces as one. The dining room doubles as a work area and can be used, too, as a dressing room. Closets on facing sides of the bedroom are outfitted for clothing and shoes. The cylinder suspended at the foot of the bed houses a television.

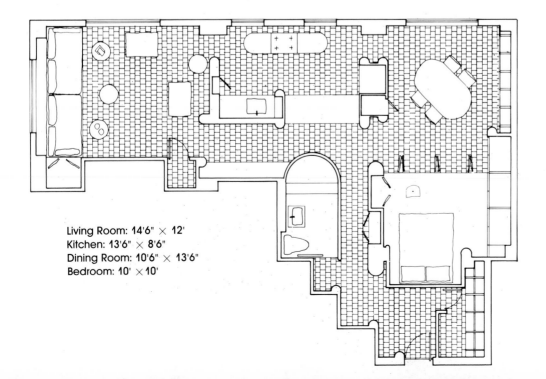

Living Room: 14'6" × 12'
Kitchen: 13'6" × 8'6"
Dining Room: 10'6" × 13'6"
Bedroom: 10' × 10'

Decorating for Comfort

They're full of charm and genteel appeal, but attached city houses, whether you know them as brownstones or row houses, are, by their very nature, tight on space. But it's just that constraint, paired with a deft decorating hand, that's responsible for making this brownstone apartment so extraordinarily engaging. Home of designer Mariette Himes Gomez and her husband, architect Raymond Gomez, it has an interior design that was dictated to a large extent by the confines of the 13-foot-wide space and the challenge of making it comfortable.

Rather than stealing precious footage to create a foyer as transition from street to shelter, Mrs. Gomez opted instead for the element of surprise: Visitors step right from the New York sidewalk into the inviting living room—a feeling, they often say, that reminds them of an English town house.

Right: Comfort to Mrs. Gomez means being surrounded by books and favorite objects, so she lined the living-room walls with built-in bookshelves and free-standing étagères, made of lacquered wood and glass, and illuminated all with down-lights slipped between the beams. To prevent the room from feeling closed in, she mirrored around the fireplace and over it hung a framed mirror so the surface wouldn't look "cold." Sofa, Breuer Wassily chairs, and see-through table of glass and Lucite, which keeps the space open visually, are centered to take advantage of the much-used fireplace.

JAMES LEVIN

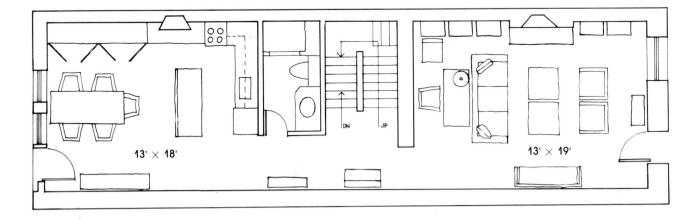

13' × 18'

13' × 19'

Opposite: Dining room and kitchen are all in one, but a separation is made—unexpectedly—by an old chest, which provides additional counter space and storage, and serves its purpose in a much more original way than a conventional counter would have. A recess to the left of the fireplace easily accommodates new storage cabinets. Mrs. Gomez chose armchairs for the French country table because she thinks they're more inviting than armless chairs. **Above:** The upstairs master bedroom's antique brass bed is monumental in size, but without a traditional tester, it doesn't appear to be. The bedspread is Victorian cutout work; the shams, Swedish antiques. **Left:** With walls and countertop covered in rich green tiles, this powder room is a little jewel that glistens when you turn on the lights. Because the room is so small and has no windows, wall-to-wall mirror was installed to give it a sense of openness.

The Built-in Solution

A wonderful location—in this case, a brownstone on a lovely New York street—and reasonable enough rent are hard to give up, even when you think you've "outgrown" a particular space. So the tenant of this tiny one-bedroom apartment, coauthor Sally Clark, asked designer Bruce Bierman to give her home a floor-to-ceiling makeover. Her requirements were an urban background for her country accessories, plus storage "everywhere." The solution is the result of a skillful pairing of coordinated over-the-counter fabrics with very functional custom storage units and built-ins.

Three major factors contribute to the apartment's new sense of spaciousness: white as an airy, unifying scheme; a tailored design throughout; and the use of just a few pieces of overscaled furniture. **Opposite:** The living-room banquette is deep enough to serve as a bed for overnight guests, and the coffee table is large enough to hold an informal dinner. Hung vertically, the prized quilt exaggerates the 14-foot ceiling of the 11-by-19-foot room. Wall-mounted lamps and an overhead track supply both focused and overall light without eating up precious floor space.

Above: Deep bins at both ends of the coffee table hold blankets and pillows. Mr. Bierman chose small graphics for all the fabrics and plastic laminates used on tables and cabinets because they're very subdued but give the eye something to look at. Laminates are Graph by Formica; fabrics are New Country Gear coordinates by Cohama/Riverdale. **Below left:** With back cushions removed, the seat cushions of the banquette become a single-size guest mattress. **Below right:** Infrequently used items can be stored in the carpeted base of the banquette.

JAMES LEVIN

JAMES LEVIN

Left top: Even though the living room is small, Mr. Bierman insisted on a permanent dining table. A table for four was installed on the wall opposite the banquette, and, because of its proximity to the closet-size kitchen (through a door to the right), it can be used for food preparation as well as dining.   **Left bottom:** To seat six, the end of the laminate-covered table flips up on its piano hinge and is supported by a cabinet that pulls out from under the counter. Most dishes and glassware are stored in these cabinets, which are kitchen-counter height along the wall so they can be used to set out an easy-to-reach buffet.

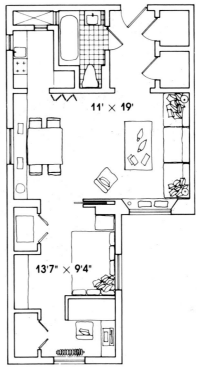

11' × 19'

13'7" × 9'4"

Opposite top left: Separated from the living/dining room by a door that slides into a wall pocket is a bedroom, 13 feet 7 inches by 9 feet 4 inches, that once had a loft bed. To make room for a "normal" bed and a permanent place to work, Mr. Bierman constructed a semi-wall that acts as a headboard for a queen-size bed, placed flush against a wall, and also divides off a zone for an office. On the opposite wall he took full advantage of the ceiling height and constructed a closet at each end with cabinets for little-used clothing above and deep bookshelves in between.   **Opposite top right:** A full-size refrigerator was installed in the bedroom closet nearest the dining room because the kitchen was too small to hold one. Large and infrequently used foods can be kept here, while the kitchen's half-refrigerator holds everyday items.   **Opposite bottom:** The desk area behind the bed, which provides ample work space, is a pleasure to use because everything is always set up but is out of sight from the rest of the apartment.

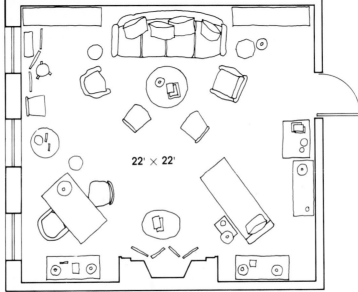

22' × 22'

One-Room Living in the Grand Manner

With its fine antique furniture and elaborate decorative painting, this one-room apartment is hardly what most of us associate with studio living. Yet the necessities are all here, from a bed to well-planned storage, proof that it's possible to have a harmonious blend of function and personal taste, no matter what the physical limitations of your space.

Measuring 22 feet square with an 11-foot ceiling, this is the home of artist/designer Richard Neas, whose objective was to create an environment that looked as if it had developed over a period of time.

Much of Mr. Neas's inspiration was Victorian and Edwardian, including the ceiling treatment, which is wallpaper with a wallpaper border. The floor, whose color gives lightness to the room, is a standard wooden parquet floor that Mr. Neas painted to simulate marble, a technique that was widely used in the 19th century. Walls are glazed red.

Opposite: "The arrangement of the furniture is somewhat unorthodox," says Mr. Neas. The desk where he works is set on an angle, and the sofa has a skirted table not to its side but directly in front of it. "It's like a tea table—a nice place to have drinks, put down a book, or pull up the chairs to have supper." The mirror and "curtain" Mr. Neas painted on it create a wonderful illusion of having more space: "It's rather like the curtains they hung in the Edwardian period between rooms, so you have the impression here you're looking into another room." The armoires were his solution for getting a lot of storage into the small space: The one on the left houses a sound system as well as storage; the one on the right, his bed. They were built with Louis XVI-style doors discovered in Paris. **Below left and**

center: The right armoire is outfitted with a Murphy bed and storage, hidden behind a shirred red curtain overhead; a reading lamp is installed on the side. The doorway at right lead to the entry, a dressing room, and a small kitchen/bar. **Below right:** Over the fireplace is a Louis XIV panel Mr. Neas found in the flea market in Paris. The engravings are his "postcards," 17th- and 18th-century handcolored prints of European cities that he's visited. Note how the fireplace panel and engravings, like the window treatments and armoires at the opposite end of the room, are brought up to the crown moldings to emphasize the room's height. The chaise longue is George I, covered in printed velvet.

Versatile Furniture for a Tiny Studio

Seven pieces of furniture were all it took for the resident of this 9-by-14-foot studio to tailor a space that would meet her every need. With a big file cabinet, bed, loveseat, table, two pull-up chairs, and a canvas screen, Trish Foley, a magazine editor, can relax, entertain, sew, read comfortably, sleep, and work at home—all without the fuss or bother of rearranging furniture.

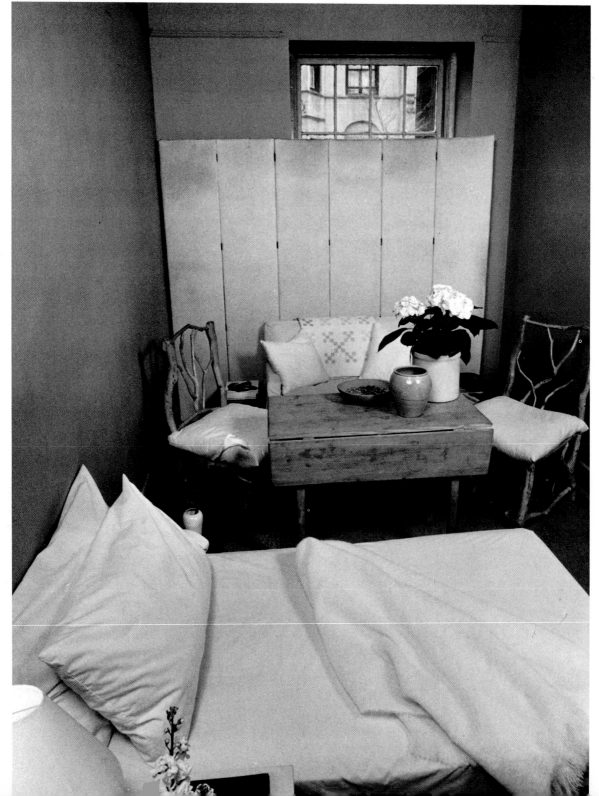

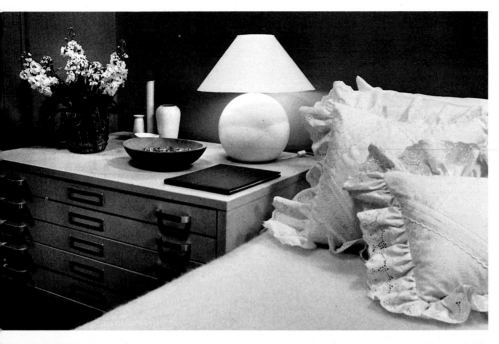

Opposite: Covered in canvas with two long pillows at its head, the bed doubles as a major piece of seating ("my interpretation of a chaise," says Miss Foley). The screen at the end of the room is also canvas, upholstered to absorb sound. She picked it to give privacy (the apartment is on the first floor) while allowing light to enter over the top. And the screen, because it is a strong horizontal element and is a paler color than the walls, makes the wall come forward and seem wider than it is.   **Left top:** A file cabinet at bedside makes the bed a convenient place to work. Drawers hold drawings, fabric samples, calculator, stationery, and so forth, and the surface is large enough to spread out books and papers.   **Left bottom:** An old Scandinavian dropleaf table, set in front of the loveseat, was chosen for its clean lines and great versatility. With a flip of its leaves, it can act as tea table, formal dining table, or even a work table for drafting or sewing.

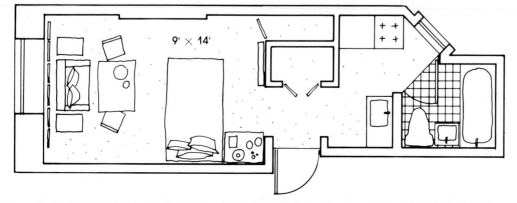

9' × 14'

A Studio with an All-Purpose Banquette

In an 11-by-13-foot studio, every inch of space has to count. So owner Stephen Granfield called on designer Mark Epstein to engineer a plan that would give him luxurious seating, a real place for dining, storage for clothes and records, *and* a full-size bed. The solution: a cleverly designed banquette/storage system that rims three walls. Some storage cabinets open like bins from the top to hold bedding and suitcases; others have drawers for clothes and for tableware; stereo components are built neatly into one end. The bed, with its channel-quilted cotton slipcover in place, slides sideways underneath one section of the cabinets to become a banquette that's the proper depth for seating, with adequate back support; an adjacent fixed section of banquette provides seating for a pull-up dining table.

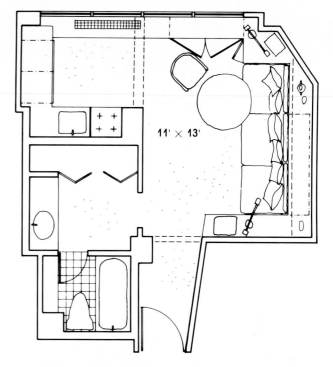

11' × 13'

Opposite top: The two-part banquette occupies the longest wall and furnishes seating for conversation and dining (the section on the right is the bed, slipped sideways under the storage cabinet). The mirror behind breaks up the mass of the wall and brings the illusion of more space into the room; in it is reflected the kitchen alcove. A shelf added above the window repeats the line of the ceiling beam, supplies a spot for books, and acts as a top surface for vertical blinds, which turn a broken-up window wall into one broad surface. The continuous stretch of one color for banquette and cabinets adds a sense of expansiveness. **Opposite bottom left:** An additional half refrigerator was placed under the counter next to the existing one to expand fresh-food storage. **Opposite bottom right:** When the bed slides out at night, its slipcover can go into a storage bin, the lamp provides good reading light, and the TV is in a convenient spot for viewing. The door visible in the mirror leads to a dressing room and bath. **Right:** Bins keep pillows at hand, can hold throw pillows and the bed's slipcover at night. Stereo components are built into the right side of the unit. All cabinets, banquette base, and bed platform are covered in matte-finished black laminate.

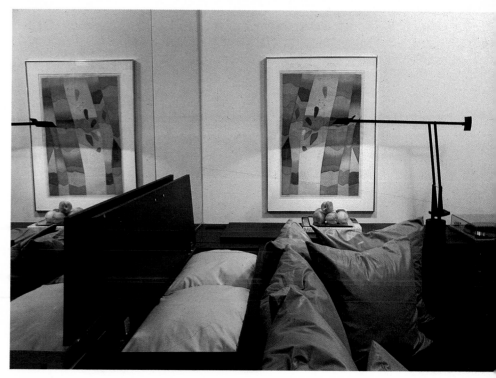

A One-Bedroom Apartment with Three Bedrooms

Take one single mother of two teenagers—one male, one female—who works at home, and how many rooms do you need? For Joan Halperin, an interior designer, the answer is only three.

The apartment in which the family lives, and she works, started out conventionally as an L-shaped living/dining room with one bedroom and a small kitchen. Now the children each have a room—the bedroom for him, the former dining area for her—and the living room acts as living room, dining room, office, and Mother's bedroom, too.

What makes this project especially exciting is that it was done fairly simply on a modest budget because the apartment is a rental and Miss Halperin (her professional name) didn't want to do any major construction. She reused everything she could, from a closet rod to a door, and all the custom cabinetry is freestanding so that it can be taken out, without damage to the apartment, should she decide to leave.

Opposite top left: All furniture in the 12-by-24-foot living room had to meet three criteria: It had to be small in scale and have lines that would contribute to a sense of spaciousness; it had to be versatile; and it had to be durable. The leather chaise had been her son's bed; since it is low and backless, Miss Halperin felt it was the perfect piece to use as a sofa by day and bed by night. Chairs are small and rounded, because curves make a space feel more open than do angles. **Opposite top right:** To give her daughter a room Miss Halperin partitioned the former living and dining areas with a cabinet topped by folding mirrored panels on tracks. The panels can be closed for privacy or opened to bring light and broader views into the living room. The bedroom, reached through the kitchen, is in the same tan-and-rose scheme as the living room for a space-expanding effect. **Opposite center left:** A 19-foot cabinet on the left wall, built in three sections and bolted together on site, combines files, drawers for clothing, and a bin for bedding. **Opposite center right:** Dining chairs are Steelcase office chairs that can be raised, lowered, or moved on their casters to suit the task at hand. The marble-topped table on recessed casters can be pulled nearer the work cabinets. **Opposite bottom left:** At night, the living/dining room becomes Miss Halperin's bedroom. **Opposite bottom right:** Miss Halperin rimmed the former master bedroom with cabinets for her teenage son's sound equipment, a desk, and drawers for his clothes and her extra files, and put heavy-duty hooks on the wall for his bicycle.

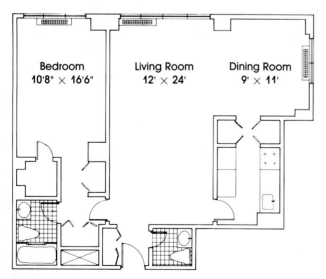

Bedroom
10'8" × 16'6"

Living Room
12' × 24'

Dining Room
9' × 11'

Before

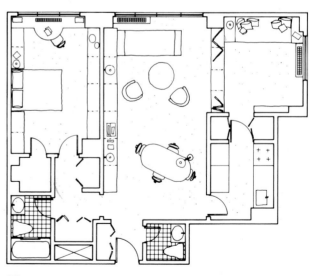

After

A Carefree Beach House

A thundering surf, blue skies, and carefree living—that's what the best of beach life is all about. When Bob Patino and Vicente Wolf approached the architectural and decorative renovation of this 1,500-square-foot house on the side of a dune, they knew that well; but they also knew how to translate good space-stretching principles into a design that is exciting and glamorous without sacrificing practicality. The key was using easy-care materials—2-inch-square tiles the color of sand, matting like that used on diving boards, and glossy white paint—and using them repetitively so that nothing breaks the space. The house is enjoyed year round by a family with children, dogs, and a great many guests.

Above: Built on stilts because of its proximity to the water, the house had several feet of open space below it. Patino/Wolf extended the siding to the ground to create space for storage and air-conditioning equipment; the front of the deck was angled so that vinyl cushions could be added for lounging. **Opposite top:** The floor and the ottoman and sofa platform bases share the same surface of matte-finished ceramic tile so that the furniture, says Mr. Patino, "is literally grounded and the space expanded because you don't see any cut-off points." The tiled platforms are on casters so they can be pushed around for parties, and the floor can be so easily mopped up that no one hesitates to walk into the house with sandy feet. The Haitian-cotton-covered cushions all have terry slipcovers, made like fitted sheets, that welcome bathing suits. At night, the mattresses can be used to sleep additional guests; bedding is stored in brushed-aluminum cylinder tables, whose tops lift off. The decks surrounding the living room and the walk to the beach are carefully lit so that the view, even at night, is extended as far as the ocean. **Right:** At the far end of the narrow living room was once a brick fireplace with a tubular flue. "The separate element broke the space," says Mr. Patino, who had it boxed in and covered with plasterboard. On the flue is one of several convex mirrors used throughout the house to turn expansive views into works of art. The pair of wire carts hold magazines indoors but can be wheeled onto the deck for serving buffets. A big space maker here is the 20-foot ceiling. "High ceilings," says Mr. Patino, "give even the smallest room the feeling of a palace." Stairs lead to two bedrooms and a bath. **Opposite bottom left:** The completely tiled fireplace cabinet divides living and dining spaces, and the side facing the table serves as storage for china. The rustic 18th-century table, chosen because it looks warm and hospitable, is the only piece of its kind in the house, yet its coloration is in tune with

its surroundings. Chairs are the dining version of the lounge chairs in the living room, another repetitive element contributing to a sense of spaciousness. **Opposite bottom right:** Diving-board matting was used extensively in the first-floor master bedroom: on floor, bed platform, and wood-trimmed storage cabinets. The photo behind the bed is from the owners' collection of fashion photography.

NORMAN McGRATH

A Simple Weekend Cabin

Like countless others scattered around lakes and mountains throughout the country, this weekend cabin was built in the simplest manner to be eminently practical. The point, after all, was not to tend house but "to get away from it all" and enjoy the site. Located on Highland Lake in New Hampshire, it is typically built of clapboard without and knotty pine paneling within and consists of two major living spaces—a screened porch for warm weather, an all-in-one room for cold—and two small bedrooms. Designer Jeri Blair and her husband, Bob, selected it for its location and decorated it to play up its homespun qualities.

Opposite top left: The cabin is a cozy spot to come home to after a long autumn walk in the woods, or after enjoying the lake for swimming and sailing in summer. **Opposite top right:** With a commanding view of the lake, the screened porch is the summer living room. A few pieces of wicker furniture keep the space feeling open, airy, and cool. **Opposite bottom:** Because the main room is used mostly in cool weather, Mrs. Blair wanted friends to step through the door and be immediately enveloped by its coziness. She therefore added beams and a plate shelf to give it more warmth and chose the kind of furniture associated with simple New England homes. Since many functions take place in the 16-by-24-foot room, Mrs. Blair selected pieces that would serve their purpose without crowding the space: The dining table and chairs blend with the paneling, so they are unobtrusive; the wing chair and rocker can be easily moved about, near the fire for reading in solitude, in front of a sofa for enjoying quiet conversations; the daybed can take care of an overnight guest. **Below top left:** The simple, functional kitchen occupies an entire wall, but because the cabinets are of the same knotty pine as the walls, it blends in without breaking up the small space. **Below bottom left:** By using bunk beds in this 9-foot-square guest room, Mrs. Blair was able to make space for an upholstered chair as well as a good-size bureau, all that are necessary to make a weekend guest feel comfortable.

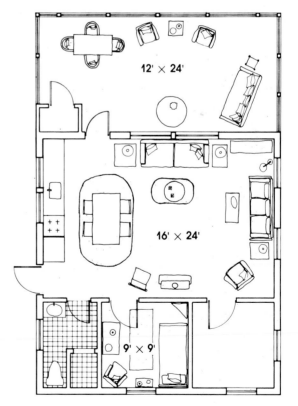

A Space-Age Cottage

The clients' request was for "a nonhouse." Their previous weekend retreat had been a heavily detailed cedar house of about 3,000 square feet. Now, they decided, they wanted a house that was basically one room and had no real furniture, a structure that didn't say "house," but rather that this was a place to eat, sleep, drink, relax. It was to be much smaller, about 1,800 square feet, and not be built of wood.

The man to whom they assigned the task was Horace Gifford, who had designed the earlier house. The material he chose for the job was Kalwall, a system of translucent fiberglass panels with insulation sandwiched within their core. Paired with large expanses of glass, it gives the simple two-story structure a futuristic face as it embraces an interior that consists of one skillfully manipulated space per floor (see plan, page 49).

Above right: The focal point of the house is the pool at its entrance. Measuring 9 feet 10 1/2 inches wide by 50 feet long, it has been incorporated into the design of the house by a system of sliding decks. In warm weather, the decks can be used as bridges over the pool for entertaining; out of season, they can cover it completely.   **Top:** The house glows from within when lights are turned on, making it an almost "otherworldly" presence on its 26-acre site. A curved greenhouse and diagonal corner windows break the structure out of a boxlike form.   **Bottom:** The dining area, with space below the table for diners' legs, occupies the center of the second story.

Opposite top: The living-room area, like the kitchen, is cantilevered over the downstairs space. The sofa Mr. Gifford designed provides all the seating and houses stereo equipment, phone jack, and television-antenna jack in one arm. The central location of the fireplace allows a single fire to be seen from the living room, dining area, and kitchen. **Opposite bottom left:** To keep the kitchen and the vista spare, all appliances, including the refrigerator and freezer, are below the countertops. On the side facing the dining table, the counter has a generous overhang for sitting comfortably on stools. **Opposite bottom right:** Sleeping spaces, bathrooms, laundry, and storage spaces occupy the ground floor. All are interconnected, yet at the same time separated, by a cleverly designed system of pocket doors, which slide into walls so they "disappear," and mirrored pivoting doors (see plan). Closets and drawers are built into the bedroom wall at left. The two-story diagonal window, like all the other glass expanses in the house, has insulated shades.

Below top and bottom: The curved greenhouse window breaks out of the box structure and brings a pair of sinks and vanities into the outdoors. This area is open to each of the two bedrooms, which are at opposite ends of the house, yet a sense of privacy can be maintained by pulling out a pocket door that divides the greenhouse space in two.

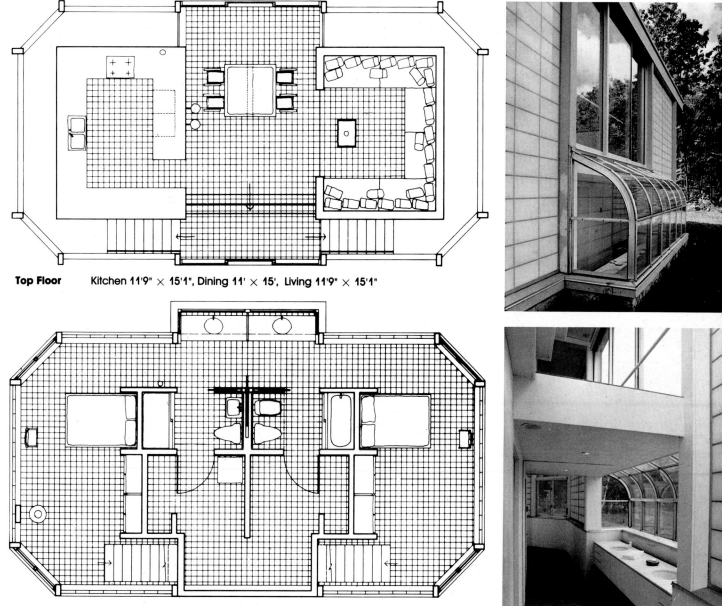

Top Floor   Kitchen 11'9" × 15'1", Dining 11' × 15', Living 11'9" × 15'1"

Ground Floor   23'3" × 42'2¹/₂"

STRETCHING FOR SPACE

Do you love the house in which you live? And all the wonderful memories that go with it? Is the neighborhood everything you've always wanted? And a place your children would be devastated to leave? If, to all of these, you answer with a resounding "yes"—and quickly follow it with, "but the house is too small"—then consider this: Are you using every inch of the house to its best advantage?

Attics are wide open for exploration and renovation. They can be the perfect place for the private master bedroom suite you've always wanted—or for giving noisy teenagers a space of their own that's far removed from the rest of family life. Skylights can fill attic rooms with sunshine, and windows on high may well capture spectacular views.

Basements, too, are terrific sources of untapped space. Playrooms, offices, media rooms, libraries, even guest rooms, can be right at home there, and still leave you extra space for laundry, workshop, sewing room, or storage.

And what about the garage? Chances are it's one of the most accessible spots in the house: just one step from the driveway and yard, and one or two from the kitchen or living room. Think about where yours is located. Is it just where you would like a bigger kitchen to be? Could you break through to an adjacent room to have a huge living space? With its wide-open interior, would it be a good playroom? Or the extra bedroom and bath that you need? If you had been contemplating an addition, it may be more practical to utilize the existing garage space and then add on a new garage or carport instead of a room.

Remember that it is generally less costly to convert existing spaces such as attics, basements, and garages than it is to add on new living space.

In this section we will show you living rooms, dining rooms, bedrooms, even a gallery for a collector, that were ingenious solutions that resulted from stretching for space.

Opposite: In a suburban Connecticut house, an attic conversion yielded sleeping space for five and a bathroom, plus this inviting reading nook, whose window overlooks a stone patio seasoned with pots of colorful flowers. The entire attic is shown on the following pages.

An Attic Opened Up to Sleep Five

Attics can offer a wealth of "undiscovered" living space. Besides being wide open by nature, and therefore easy to divide the way you want, they probably have windows to catch superb views you never knew you had.

Finding this one-story suburban Connecticut house somewhat cramped for their family of five, the owners decided that the likely direction to move was up. A staircase, located at one end of the living room, now reaches up to a spacious second floor that houses a master bedroom with a big walk-in closet, a family bathroom, a large room with plenty of space for the three girls to sleep and play, plus an added bonus: a cozy hallway library at the top of the stairs.

Above: Stairs ascend to the center of the space, treated as a library, with bath and master bedroom to the right, children's room to the left. **Opposite top left:** In the master bedroom, simple painted wood was used effectively to keep the room's lines spare while supplying adequate storage. Television and cabinets take advantage of the otherwise useless low areas created here by the pitch of the roof. Skylight is located to bathe the room, but not the bed, in light. Stairs lead to a big walk-in closet. **Opposite top right:** In the bathroom, a huge skylight supplies wonderful natural light and also allows bathers the headroom needed to stand when getting in and out of the tub. The toilet is behind the partial wall. **Opposite bottom left:** A spot of their own for snacking or playing fits cozily under the low-ceilinged area in the children's room. Three identical configurations of Palaset cubes hold their clothes. The youngest's crib is in this area. **Opposite bottom right:** One long shelf is work and play surface for the two older girls, whose beds are tucked into the low-ceilinged area on the higher level. Under the shelf, Palaset storage cubes keep toys and art supplies neat and organized. Used on the ceiling, striped Marimekko wallpaper emphasizes the room's height.

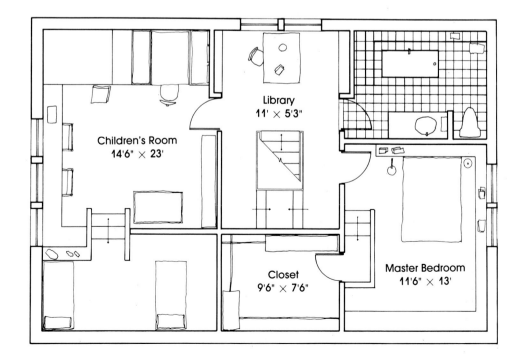

Children's Room
14'6" × 23'

Library
11' × 5'3"

Closet
9'6" × 7'6"

Master Bedroom
11'6" × 13'

JAMES LEVIN

A Basement Gallery and Game Room

An important collection of American folk art had outgrown the house; three teenage boys needed room for a noisy game of table tennis. The only space left was the basement, a typical maze of exposed concrete blocks, pipes, ducts, beams, and columns. Designer Robert K. Lewis enclosed as much structural work as possible with a dropped ceiling and rough-sawn wood walls, then painted all an unexpected bright white. Flooring is taupe quarry tile.

Left: Instead of using a conventional green table, Mr. Lewis designed one that would be more decorative and more functional. In white plastic laminate with maple inlays, it divides at the net into two parts that can be separated for cards or party dining. Folding chairs are kept in a closet. **Below:** Display shelves with storage below are a perfect example of how good design deals successfully with existing problems: This exaggerated waterfall treatment satisfies the owners' needs while masking an irregular wall created by the house's foundation.

Room over the Garage

One of a house's great unsung sources of potential space is something most people overlook: the top portion of the garage. "In the fifties and sixties, many builders put up high garages to be in scale with the architecture of the two-story houses they were building," points out Alan Shope of Shope Reno Wharton architects, who recently tapped the leftover space in this Greenwich, Connecticut, house.

The clients had been contemplating an addition for a family room, but the architects considered their budget unrealistic for major new construction. The garage, however, fit all the criteria for being adapted: It held two cars and was high enough so that the space would be workable; the structure was sound; and its location was perfect—right next to the kitchen.

Using a garage is a good alternative to an addition if (1) you want to keep costs down, (2) you are too close to your property line to build an acceptable addition, or (3) you're concerned about altering your house's architecture. In this case, the only clue to the change inside is a large new window designed to keep the facade from looking bland.

Opposite top: The architects felt the space needed both a vertical and a lateral thrust and wanted more than a typical cathedral ceiling, so they devised an arched ceiling (built of plywood) and designed a window that mirrors its curve. Because the window is opposite the entry stairs from the kitchen, it gives the room an anchor. It also provides a view of a beautiful pond, which the owners had not been able to see before; the window juts out so that there is a window seat. **Opposite bottom left and right:** To each side of the central entry stairway is a light well that was designed to bring light into the room while keeping the skylight out of sight. One closet is used for storage (not shown) and the other for sewing. When the sewing closet's doors are open, there's plenty of light and space for working; when finished, the owner can close the doors and everything disappears.

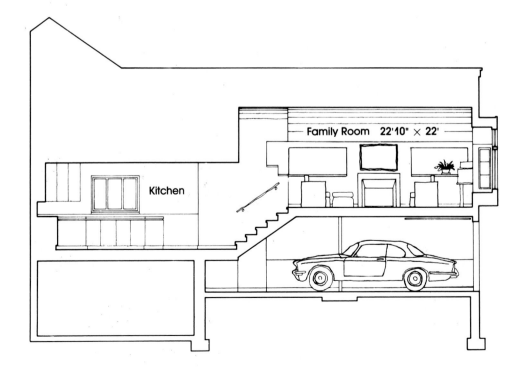

Kitchen

Family Room 22'10" × 22'

Den/Dining Room/Kitchen Created from a Garage

The location was superb, the house too small. The perfect solution: stretching into the garage. A garage, after all, offers a large amount of generally unobstructed space, has convenient access to the rest of the house, and, an important point not to be overlooked, is a fine fit architecturally. By rethinking that existing space, the owners of this once-dark house have today a sun-filled dining area, an efficient new kitchen, and an informal family room, all with wonderful outdoor views.

Below top: With its original garage converted to living space, the house retains its conventional form; the breezeway, which now has floor-to-ceiling windows, was incorporated into a new living room made by uniting the old utility room, kitchen, and dining room. Landscaping and a stockade fence give the front yard privacy, so designer Robert K. Lewis was able to replace the garage door with a 12-foot-high greenhouse wall that makes the 11-by-11-foot dining area behind it seem much larger than it is. A new garage was added to the right of the old one. **Opposite:** Because the kitchen is open to both the dining area and the family room, Mr. Lewis made it as clutter-free as possible. An overhead cabinet holds a plugged-in toaster oven; an under-counter drawer slides out to reveal a food processor at a convenient height for working; and a pantry closet has a counter-height shelf for an electric coffee maker. **Below bottom left and right:** The family room (seen here from the living room) is actually located in a 10-foot-wide strip that was added along the entire back of the house. A convenient bar cabinet backs up to the kitchen. Glasses are in the overhead cabinet, liquor bottles in a deep drawer over the wine rack, bar tools and mixers in the under-sink cabinet.

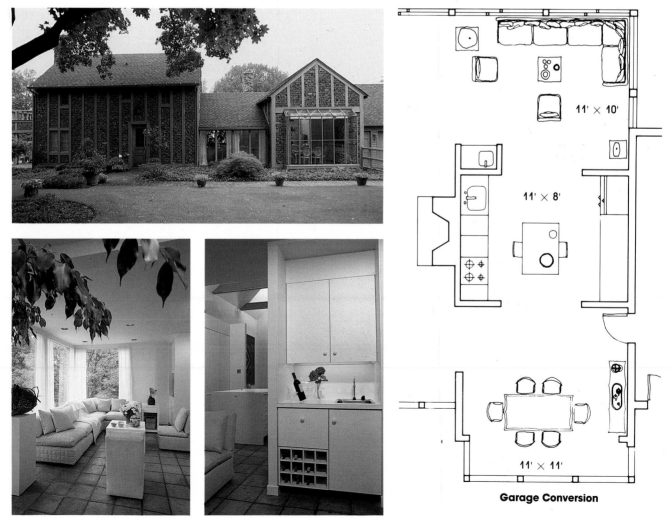

11' × 10'

11' × 8'

11' × 11'

Garage Conversion

A Garage Expansion Yields a Living Room

With soaring ceiling, seating for 20, and a formidable collection of American folk art, this 16-by-36-foot living room is the highlight of a once-undistinguished builder's house on Long Island, New York. It came into being when the owners, a couple with three teenagers, decided they had outgrown the house as it was (the living room, which stopped behind the long sofa in the foreground of the room, seated four or five) and that they liked the neighborhood too much to move. So they set their sights on the adjacent garage, combined it with the modest living room, and called on designer Robert K. Lewis to detail the interior.

Right: Mr. Lewis raised the roof of the whole space to form a tray ceiling, framed it with beams, and created "skylights" by inserting blinds into some of the sections to admit light from clerestory windows behind them.
Below: Focal point of the major seating area is a fireplace and storage wall of touch-latch cabinets made from 18th-century French oak paneling with an American pine mantel, circa 1810. It was designed to minimize the depth of the newly added firebox while at the same time creating a place to "hide" a television (bottom left), videocassette recorder (top left), and other items.

JAMES LEVIN

A Wide-Open Kitchen in a Former Garage

There's room for cooking with ease, for dining with friends as well as family, and for enjoying much-loved collections of cookware and tableware, all because the owners of this suburban Connecticut house saw the possibilities of a garage. What makes this conversion so special is the way the owners dealt with the space: Instead of redoing the exterior to make the garage look like part of the house, they recognized that the garage's design was integral to the whole. So they used the space "as is," and got the added bonus of car-size doors that swing wide open to allow the pleasures of indoors and out to mingle.

Above top and bottom: This garage was used as a work space by the previous owners, who added a garage for cars at right. In summer, it's a delight to leave the doors open when cooking. **Left:** Adding beams reinforced the nature of the kitchen's beginnings as unfinished space. The table is a sheet of plywood, on legs, for which the owners made fabric covers that slip on like contour sheets.

JAMES LEVIN

NEW-STYLE HOUSING

Something has happened to housing in the last couple of decades. With most of the major costs affecting building steadily rising, builders have been investigating the only possible solution—going smaller—with a lot of very exciting results. Suddenly we find ourselves with a whole new "house" vocabulary: cluster, attached, modular, patio, studio, shared or tandem (as in "a house shared by tandem buyers"), and, of course, town house (even when it's in the country). Not to mention quadruplex, sexplex, and octoplex. There are more condominium and cooperative apartments (high-rise and otherwise) than you might ever have thought possible. Plus apartments being carved out of ordinary houses and out of grand old mansions, and those being creatively constructed in buildings originally intended for commercial use. Some are entirely new forms of housing; others are the result of rethinking and recycling the old.

Does that alter your concept of "home" as you know it? It doesn't have to. There are adobe town houses in the Southwest, barns converted to apartments in the Midwest, and Colonial villages in the Northeast that evoke strong senses of regionalism. In many areas, stately old mansions are being broken into smaller units, saving the splendid buildings while at the same time allowing apartments to slip effortlessly into the fiber of single-house neighborhoods. Sometimes the grounds are recycled as well, with clusters of attached housing around the property.

Among the new breeds of housing are homes with two (or more) separate-but-equal master bedrooms that allow unrelated people to live privately within a single structure whose common spaces (and expenses) they share; freestanding houses that, like studio apartments, are basically one multifunctional space; apartments that offer the excitement of living in a one-time schoolhouse, an old textile mill, or even a former church.

On the next pages we take a look at some of the options and at how their residents are living today in new-style housing.

Opposite: Created as a prototype for shared living, this house by architect Barry Berkus of Berkus Group Architects offers two master bedrooms and many amenities in 1,336 square feet of space, including a loft. A 16-foot arch creates an important-looking entryway and is an invitation to enter through the patio, where the house really begins. More on the house on the following pages.

A House Built for Shared Living

If there is one house that speaks to new housing needs of the 1980s, it may well be this. Designed as a prototype for the home-building industry, it is low in square footage (969 square feet with a 154-square-foot loft, plus 213 square feet in a detached office/bedroom) but looks much larger; high on amenities (decks, outdoor fireplace and whirlpool tub, a greenhouse); affordable (about $35 per square foot in Southern California); and geared to the burgeoning market for a new phenomenon known as a shared house. Also known as a tandem house, a shared house is defined as one with two (or more) private sleeping spaces and communal living spaces. Included in this market are singles buying to divide a mortgage; divorced parents with teenage children; elderly people with companions who live in to help them or to contribute rent; and couples needing an "in-law apartment."

The aims of this shared house are to show how space-stretching ideas can make a compact design feel much larger than it is and to provide today's buyers with a home that doesn't skimp on amenities. Conceived as an experimental house by *Housing* magazine, it was designed by architect Barry Berkus, whose California-based Berkus Group Architects is a leader in smaller, high-density housing design, and decorated by Jack Childs and Gene Dreyfus of The Childs/Dreyfus Group in Chicago.

Its basic plan can be adapted to different climates, sites, and densities, and the prototype is already making an impact: Versions are being built all over the United States, both on city lots and in vacation spots. Here's how it was made to live big.

Right top: The patio extends the house by being an outdoor living space, complete with whirlpool spa, fireplace, and a wet bar with icemaker. • Although open, the deck is raised so it can't be seen by passersby; and because it is private, the house opens to it, creating an expansive feeling. **Opposite:** Light, volume, and an emphasis on vertical space create a feeling of great openness in the 13-foot-wide living room. • The eye is drawn up by a loft, light from a skylight and 10-foot window at rear, and a ceiling fan. • Track lights and recessed fixtures were used instead of freestanding lamps, which would have broken up the space. • See-through coffee tables disappear visually. • Mirror and lighting under the sofa and the wall-hung cabinet on the right wall make the furniture appear to float. • The mirrored back of the kitchen island and the mirrored ceiling overhead bounce the light around and erase boundaries.

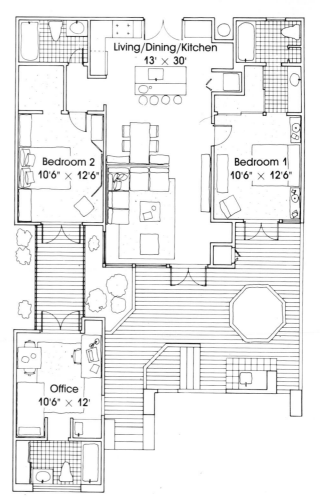

Living/Dining/Kitchen
13' × 30'

Bedroom 2
10'6" × 12'6"

Bedroom 1
10'6" × 12'6"

Office
10'6" × 12'

Top left and right: The well-planned kitchen has room for a 25.7-cubic-foot refrigerator, range with plug-in griddle and grill, overhead microwave oven that incorporates a pull-out glass hood for the grill, a pantry closet, and a washer/dryer unit. • Glass doors on the pantry closet and overhead cabinets open the space to its maximum (solid doors would cut off about a foot visually). • The raised section of the kitchen counter can be used for informal meals. • Double doors lead to a greenhouse, creating an open feeling in the kitch-en. **Bottom left and right:** For maximum privacy, the two master bedrooms, each about 11 X 13 feet with a bath, are on opposite sides of the living room. • In-doors and out were combined to make master bed-room number one (left) feel bigger: French doors extend the room to the deck; exterior siding on the wall behind the bed brings the outside in. • Mirror lightens the mass of the queen-size bed. • In the sec-ond master bedroom (right), a pair of armoires flanking the double bed supply plentiful storage.

Above: A dramatic skylight tops the walkway that connects the second master bedroom with the detached office/bedroom, which is also accessible directly from the house's front entry deck. **Right top and bottom:** Although it's only 11 feet from the second bedroom, there is a great sense of privacy in the detached space, which can be used as a bedroom, recreation room, cabana (it's not far from the whirlpool), or, as it is here, an office with hideaway guest bed. • A high ceiling stretches the space. • A wet bar on the left rear wall is useful in this kind of situation, but a compact kitchen could also fit in this space to make the room completely self-sufficient. • On the right rear wall, a twin-size Sico folding bed lets the space function as a guest room. • A see-through table, which takes up no space visually, can be used for conferences or dining.

Home Sweet Home in an Old Filling Station

The situation of this one-room house couldn't be more 20th-century or urban: It's a former gas station located on a busy corner of New York's Greenwich Village. But the environment within looks as if it came straight from one of the original 13 Colonies. That's because its owner, Hoen Meiers, a long-time collector of American antiques, decided it would be fitting to treat the space like a traditional one-room house: No hidden beds, no dining tables that disappear, just straightforward furniture that serves the purpose for which it was intended.

Left: The stark exterior has newly added, traditional-looking small-paned windows. **Opposite top:** Living as if he were in Colonial New England, Mr. Meiers uses very little upholstered furniture. The room measures 18 by 30 feet with a jog that is the bathroom. **Opposite bottom left:** Because the building had no ceiling, Mr. Meiers installed one, with recessed lighting for gentle overall light. The wood-burning stove supplies all heat. **Opposite bottom right:** A tavern table serves as a cozy dining spot. Kitchen shelves display American stoneware, and the counter opposite, high enough on the dining side to shield its sink from diner's view, acts as a storage pantry.

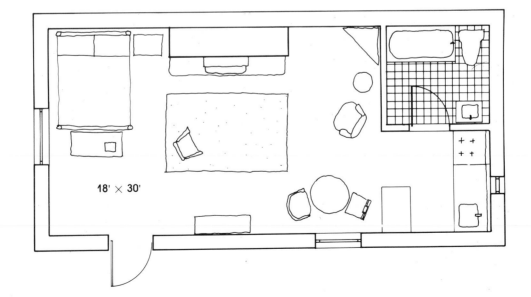

18' × 30'

An Apartment Carved from Commercial Space

Old textile mills, garages, factories, even big churches—they're all part of today's trend of converting no-longer-used properties into interesting residential buildings. Often they're divided into lofts with wide-open floor plans that allow the residents to mold the space as they see fit; other times, their idiosyncrasies dictate the floor plans. What many of them have in common, however, is odd, irregularly shaped spaces that can be awkward if not handled properly.

Typical of the kinds of buildings being converted across the country is this trio of former parking garages in Brooklyn, New York, which architect Leonard Colchamiro transformed into a 54-unit apartment building known as the Atrium. When

Barbara Ross and Barbara Schwartz of Dexter Design were called in to decorate the apartment shown here, they were struck by how the architect had maximized what might have been a disadvantage—irregular space—and made it into an advantage: "Instead of a sterile box to live in," says Mrs. Ross, "you get interesting environments: varied levels, room sizes, ceiling heights, window arrangements, and something unusual and remarkable to live with." The plan that Dexter Design devised for this particular space takes advantage of the duplex apartment's open floor plan and incorporates a sense of more conventional separated spaces into it, a concept that can be easily adapted in similar places.

Opposite top: One reason these kinds of unique spaces are so appealing is that they present many options. In this large downstairs room, it was decided to create three environments that would each have their privacy without losing the advantage of the open floor plan. The solution was to use a low Y-shaped partition, built of Sheetrock, that would allow people seated in each area to feel secluded; when they are standing, however, they can see from one area to the next. The section to the right is a TV/entertainment area; the one to the left, a home office/library. At the rear is a pool table with a seating area where a guest could spend

the night on a convertible sofa. Partition walls are painted a different color facing each space. **Opposite bottom:** The upstairs living room and dining area take full advantage of the open floor plan and were treated as one comfortable environment, but unlike the practice in many conversions today, the kitchen is in a distinctly separate area (located at the rear), instead of being in the middle of the space, so the cook can work out of the view of guests. The living/dining room is painted pink and decorated with burgundies, magentas, some russet and black; furniture and floors are light woods.

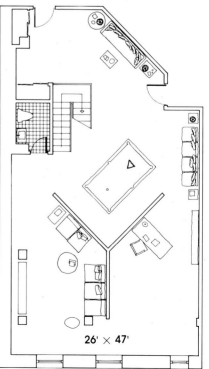

26' × 47'

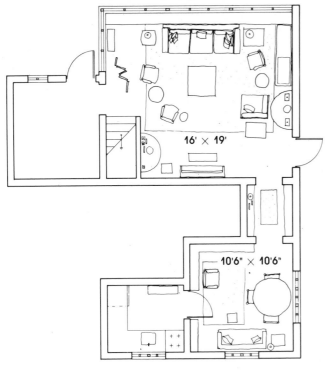

16' × 19'

10'6" × 10'6"

An Artist's Studio for Full-Time Living

A decorative painter and fabric designer, Francis Dearden lives in what seems for him a likely choice: an artist's studio. But this is a studio that was intended for working only, a place where walls of windows would shed their light on sculptures in progress. Somewhat ahead of its time, it was built about 40 years ago of cinder block with factory windows. But Mr. Dearden has chosen to live here today in a gracious manner, creating within the industrial-looking building a very personal environment that enchants the eye by giving it an enormous amount to look at, even in its smallest rooms.

dustrial windows, and a charming collection of animal forms makes the room immensely personal. **Left top:** Originally part of a farm, the studio was built for the owner's wife and sits on a grassy knoll above a root cellar. **Left bottom:** Instead of being confined by the tiny size of his kitchen, Mr. Dearden keeps much of his kitchenware in the open. When he recently noticed a chip in the paint of the base cabinet on the far wall, Mr. Dearden painted a pheasant right over it. Now the pheasant's shadow adds a sense of dimension to the space. **Above:** This 9-by-12-foot room has many faces: dining room, den for reading the morning paper and perusing cookbooks, showplace of a majolica collection assembled over 20 years. Because he has plenty of privacy, Mr. Dearden devised open window treatments that extend his view to the outdoors. This rope-draped bamboo rod, grapevine wreath, and copper mold have a greenhouse and trees as a backdrop.

Opposite top and bottom right: A two-story ceiling and a wall of glass expand the 24-foot-square living room and make it feel spacious and airy. At the same time, Mr. Dearden has injected it with a great sense of comfort and coziness. Curtains frame the massive in-

A Pied-à-Terre in a Servant's Room

Years ago, they were servants' rooms—small cubicles with minimal facilities, located at a distance from the employers' apartments, often in basements or on roofs. Today these orphan spaces are typical of the unusual, and now often desirable, spaces with which city dwellers are faced.

Located in a prime residential neighborhood in New York City, this former rooftop maid's room is blessed with a view and serves now as a luxurious pied-à-terre. Because the owners use it mainly for themselves, designer Mariette Himes Gomez concentrated on furniture that would make their visits wonderfully comfortable. There's a real bed instead of a convertible sofa, upholstered furniture for lounging, an intimate-size dining table, and a kitchen that hides behind louvered doors, all in 288 square feet of space.

Opposite top and bottom left: To make the most of the interior space, a windowed dining area was "pushed out" onto the rooftop. Raising the area on a platform gave it a sense of separation and a better view, too. A wicker table and chair are positioned by the banquette for family meals but can be folded up and put away when the banquette is needed to seat a crowd at an informal gathering. Because their daughter sometimes accompanies them to the city, the clients requested plenty of sleeping space. The solution was a queen-size bed with a convertible sofa at its foot. A futon is also kept handy to sleep an additional guest. **Below left and right:** To use up the least amount of floor space, the entire kitchen, a 4-foot-wide unit that incorporates sink, range, and refrigerator, was installed directly behind bifold doors so the cook actually stands in the living area when working.

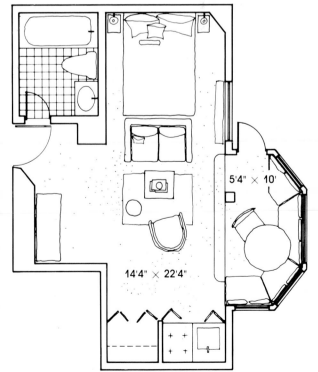

5'4" × 10'

14'4" × 22'4"

An Apartment in a Suburban House

This colorful clapboard house in a New England suburb has taken on a new life: Its interior has been carved into four apartments, preserving an exterior that fits into the neighborhood and providing its new residents with a taste of the life-style that makes this house-oriented community so appealing. At the house's peak is a tiny three-room apartment whose considerable charm and affordable rent made it a fine choice for a young couple, Albert Turick and his wife, Chris Shearer, both of whom are in the design field. Inexpensive do-it-yourself cosmetic work gave them the space they needed, and a home that looks special.

Right: An outside stairway and deck give this upstairs apartment a private entrance. **Opposite top:** Because the living room measures only 10 by 14 feet, Mr. Turick did not want to break it up with a lot of furniture. He therefore constructed a 4-inch-high platform that simplifies the space two ways: It ties all of the room's wooden elements together as one "piece" of furniture, and, at the same time, it obscures the green carpet beneath so that now there are only two surfaces, one white and one beige. The banquette he built uses up little of the precious floor space yet has room for a useful shelf behind it. The platform serves another function as well—by stopping it 30 inches from the front door, Mr. Turick was able to define a separate entrance foyer within the space (see how it works through the bedroom door on the following pages). **Opposite bottom:** Adding a small platform to match the one on the floor made this bookcase a more substantial piece of furniture. A table for two set on the deck outside the picture window serves as additional summer living space and, by drawing the eye outside, visually expands the interior.

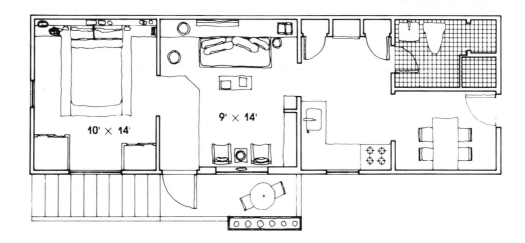

10' × 14'

9' × 14'

Above: With very little closet space and no room for a bureau, the bedroom called for construction and ingenuity, too. Baskets on the shelf hold underwear and socks; inexpensive clamp-on lights supply reading light unobtrusively. A view into the living room shows how the new platform was used to define an entry foyer.
Right: Every inch of the bed's platform was put to work. There's one large storage compartment under the mattress and three more bordering it, each with a lift-up top (a wide stick props up the mattress).

Space, and not having enough of it, is a problem affecting all of us these days, no matter who we are, no matter how small or large our home, or how small or large our decorating budget. Says one interior designer who caters to an upscale market, "Every single client we deal with has a space problem of some kind, whether it's finding enough storage, having room for guests, or making sure the living room is efficient for entertaining, dining, and relaxing."

- Do you need a place for formal sit-down dinner parties but have no formal dining room?
- Would you like your two children each to have privacy, but what you have is one bedroom that they must share?
- Is it important that you have a quiet office at home, but you can't find a place to put one?

This section is geared to helping you solve the problem. It is arranged, therefore, not by actual rooms but by domestic needs. If it's a spot you want for an overnight guest, for example, you would look under Sleeping Spaces—and may find that your answer rests in the living room, library, or even the home office. Similarly, if it's a grandly decorated boudoir you long for (and your bedroom is an 8-by-10-foot white box), or if you want to accommodate your wardrobe in a closetless bedroom, you will find suggestions for solving those problems under Sleeping Spaces as well.

This section will assist you in several different ways: by helping you find possible locations, such as an inventive place for dining; physically create spaces you need where none exists; manipulate small spaces to work better and look bigger; and see how to put together a particular look you want in a small space.

Our intent is not to show you every possibility in the world, but to open your mind to the infinite options, and to show you approaches that may inspire your own creative solutions.

Many solutions are the result of inspired design; still others come from the use of inventive products. Following this section, beginning on page 192, is a portfolio of readily available products that address particular problems: furniture and appliances that are scaled down to take up less space; ingenious multipurpose furniture, such as a round ottoman that hides a bed inside; imaginative storage pieces, such as a sleek, low cabinet from which a television rises; unique problem-solvers such as a free-standing coat closet; and much more.

THREE

ZEROING IN ON SPACES

LIVING SPACES

The living space is what most of us address first: the room that greets the public and tells them about us as we are, or as we would like to be. A room's dimensions, as the next pages will show you, are no limitation. The smallest of rooms can be utterly grand; and small rooms, too, can accommodate with superb style the bits and pieces with which we like to surround ourselves. In many cases, living spaces are the ones we choose for serving many functions: cooking and eating as well as socializing; sleeping and working as well as entertaining. These many needs can be catered to in limited space as well. It's all a matter of thoughtful design.

Overscaled Furniture for Impact

One surefire way to pack drama into a space is to take the bold approach. A few well-designed pieces of overscaled furniture used in a pared-down arrangement quickly simplify a room and create an inherent sense of spaciousness. Pair that with strong color, and even a space bereft of architectural embellishments takes on an importance that belies its beginnings.

Although this room had the benefit of a 16-foot ceiling in one area, it was very dark and was filled with eccentric beams and jogs resulting from the building's recent conversion from offices to apartments. When Robert K. Lewis approached its interior design, he took his cue from the 60-year-old building's Egyptian facade and chose a rich terracotta color, furniture, and decorative devices that would recall its classical spirit.

Opposite: Key to the simplified furniture arrangement is one long banquette at dining height. It serves as seating both for the table and for lounging, and, at the same time, exaggerates the length of the wall on which it's placed. Both this banquette and the one at the end of the room are deep and luxurious, but because they're the same color as the walls, their bulk is minimized. At the far end of the room, a banquette stretches the width of a newly created tiled platform to abut a window at each end, making it feel almost like an outdoor space. To play up the loggia effect, Mr. Lewis added a pair of imposing columns, which are in reality cardboard tubes painted with a rough sand finish to resemble stone. The wall appears to be massive blocks of rosy marble, but it is actually a clever illusion by decorative painter Robert Jackson.   **Right:** Because the dining table is situated under a lowered ceiling (there is a media loft above), it enjoys a sense of intimacy within the larger space. The table is a slab of rose-colored marble on a brass pedestal; the chairs, copies of antiquities made in walnut with leather-thonged seats topped by cushions.

Grand Design on a Small Scale

With its regal forms and elegant air, this living room has all the grandeur of a European salon. But it is, in fact, a somewhat conventional-size room in a small New York brownstone, a truly amazing decorating feat performed by its resident, interior designer John Robert Moore II. What Mr. Moore has done is take advantage of the 18-by-20-foot room's generous 11-foot ceiling height and, by using low, scaled-down furniture, emulated the proportions we associate with grand rooms. The silver paper he chose for the walls reflects light in a gentle, gracious manner and seems to make the perimeters of the room disappear. Mirror, a much "harder" reflective surface, is used sparingly: on the sides of the niche behind the sofa, for shutters that take the place of curtains, and as ornamental medallions that are hung like paintings. Rich, unusual colors heighten the sense of luxury, as does the floor painted by artist Robert Jackson to evoke images of the crackled surface of aged porcelain.

Platforms and Buffet Make Room for a Crowd

Entertaining on a grand scale, listening to favorite music comfortably, even sleeping a couple of overnight guests—all are possible in one room with careful space planning. A case in point: this living room designed by Mark Epstein for John Gutierrez. The key is the clever use of platforms and a buffet that look built in, but are actually freestanding. In addition to giving the room architectural interest, the 10-inch-high, 32-inch-deep platforms that rim the walls provide plenty of informal seating, and also incorporate the "sofas," two twin mattresses lined lavishly with pillows so that they have a comfortable seating depth. The buffet that neatly holds stereo components and records is also a fine spot for setting out food because it's next to the dining table.

Four Steps to Creating Spaciousness

It was a rather ordinary 14-by-21-foot living room with nothing interesting about it. No architecture, no molding, no fireplace. Windows that were too small. And a beam at the top of one wall that, when the opposite wall was mirrored, would be reflected and make the room feel even longer and narrower than it was. But by taking four important steps, its resident, designer Tom O'Toole, has made a significant transformation. "Now the main attraction of the room," he says, "is a feeling of space—and it's all an illusion." Here's how he did it.

One: The offending beam on the right-hand wall was done away with by building a new wall flush with the beam (photo below). Although the room lost about 4 inches in width, it now seems higher because the wall is unbroken.

Two: To make the windows feel bigger, and to hide a radiator, window air conditioner, and speakers, Mr. O'Toole devised a window treatment that consists of floor-length matchstick blinds and curtains that exaggerate the height and width of the windows while masking the mechanical elements.

PETER LOPPACHER

The diagonal stripes of the curtain fabric repeat the vertical ones of the Marimekko wallpaper, which make the room seem higher.

Three: Mirroring one long side of the rectangular room made the wall "disappear" to create the illusion of a large, square room. The deception is aided by the large, wall-hugging sofa that, when reflected, emphasizes the two outer boundaries of the room, one real and one imagined. Note how the half-round table against the mirror "melts" into its reflection and appears to be a large round table.

Four: Upholstered furniture was chosen to visually stretch the room. Modular seating always gives you the most seating in a space, but here Mr. O'Toole used it for another purpose as well: Extending it as far toward the entry door as possible (photo above) makes the room seem larger than it is. The pieces are low for the same reason; their fabric was vertically channel-quilted to hide the divisions between the three sections, thereby making them seem like one long, continuous piece.

Quick-Change Decorating

The luxury of "winter rooms" and "summer rooms" may be a thing of the past, but it's still a pleasure to have a visual change of pace, especially in limited living space.

Slipcovers are a long-favored vehicle for decorators, who know how a switch from a hardy fabric such as cotton duck to a more elaborate flowered chintz can take a room from contemporary to traditional in a matter of minutes. But a transformation doesn't have to be as costly: A simple switching of accessories such as pillows, blankets, and even flowers can give a room a sprightly lift. Here are very different rooms that afford their residents two looks in one space.

Left: Strong florals are the focal point in this English-style sitting room designed by Harry Schule and Ned Marshall. They're used for upholstery, throw pillows, window treatments, and the area rug, too. **Below:** Here, solid colors, used for slipcovers and window treatments, give the room a decidedly contemporary air. For additional freshness, some of the furniture and accessories are changed as well.

Above: This small, neutral-colored living space designed by Joseph Lembo gets its seasonal change with accessories. In autumn and winter, the throw pillows are a mix of taupe and butterscotch, and a luxurious fringed throw warms the banquette.   **Left:** In spring and summer, the throw is removed and the pillows are a lighthearted mix of tan and white stripes punctuated with solid turquoise.

Room for Furniture, Objects, and Friends

Here's a room that defies the principle that the less you have in a space, the more expansive it feels. Its rich look and unique charm come not so much from fine furniture and accessories—though it has those, too—as it does from deft decorating and the layering upon layering of very personal objects. Most actually belong to English-born decorator Keith Irvine, from mementos from the British royal family to a Pooh bear to part of a bishop's coat used as a table skirt. The room was designed by Mr. Irvine and his partner, Thomas Fleming, of Irvine and Fleming, for the Kips Bay Show House in the manner of an "upstairs sitting room," and though the space measures but 11 feet 6 inches by 22 feet, there are ample places to seat 10 or 12.

Right: Mr. Irvine and Mr. Fleming are known for high-style rooms that look well-worn and comfortable, just as if the family had lived in them forever. Here's how they were able to create the look in just over 250 square feet of space. • Because the room was long and narrow, they "widened" it by using mirror on the chimney breast and opposite wall. "The mirrors also pick up every bit of movement—people, curtains blowing in the breeze, the glitter of candlelight—and make the space seem bigger," says Mr. Fleming. • Objects were hung all the way up the wall to emphasize the ceiling height. • The richness of very fine pieces of furniture, including the Louis XVI bergère and the two Thomas Hope chairs at the backgammon table by the window, was tempered and "relaxed" by furniture such as the worn painted wicker chair and "a simple, falling-away background" created with tatami wall covering edged in split bamboo, and straw matting on the floor. • "The curtain treatment is much more elaborate, to stand up to the black Regency cornice," says Mr. Fleming, "but we had only one window to work with. It might not be so elaborate if we had three." • A club chair and ottoman were used because they have the look of a chaise but add seating flexibility; the ottoman can be moved around and two people seated.

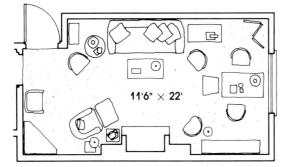

11'6" × 22'

JAMES LEVIN

94

Three Rooms Out of Two

With a 12½-by-28-foot living room and a separate 10½-by-12-foot dining room, this apartment had plenty of space, but not the particular spaces the clients wanted. By rethinking the apartment's traditional layout, designer Mark Epstein was able to give them a living room and dining room *plus* a den with room for overnight guests.

First step was eliminating a hallway and creating an opening between the large living room and the dining room to make the two spaces flow together. With pocket doors installed, the former dining room is now a den that can be closed off when guests spend the night on its sofa bed.

Key to reworking the living room so that it could accommodate dining without sacrificing precious floor space was the ingenious selection of furniture: A banquette with seating on both sides of a common back serves both the dining table and the living room, eliminating the "dead space" that would have resulted from using more conventional arrangements.

JAMES LEVIN

Below: Three spaces (and four functions) where once there were two: Dining and conversational areas are in the former living room; the den/guest room at right was the dining room. **Opposite bottom:** A sculptural ceiling structure with recessed lighting, viewed here from the conversation area, repeats the lines of the two-sided banquette and defines the areas in the room.
Left: The den/guest room sofa, which faces a storage wall with built-in television (not shown), opens to sleep two. The mirror lining the wall between the top and bottom rows of cabinets reflects the living room and gives the den an illusion of additional depth.

One Room, Three Zones

In the beginnings of this country, people lived in one room out of necessity. But as we became more affluent, cooking facilities and beds were pushed out and the living space became a room of its own. "But now we've become more interested in food and cooking," says Charles Mount, known for his kitchen and restaurant designs, "and we're going back to a one-room experience, which unites cooking and living spaces, on a grand scale." The space that Mr. Mount designed for himself is the union of three small rooms and was conceived as a wide-open loft with a kitchen at its heart. "To me, this is the most interesting way to partake in everything I enjoy."

Opposite top: By removing walls and combining three small rooms into a 26-by-35-foot one with living/dining/cooking zones, Mr. Mount created the illusion of more space. White walls and white-limed oak floors keep the room open and airy. **Opposite bottom left:** The banquette supplies plentiful seating with cabinets for speakers and storage at its ends. Visual interest comes from a mix of textures, all in shades of brown—hand-loomed mohair-and-wool carpet for the base; channeled goat's-hair fabric for the seat pillows; linen for the back pillows; a black-striped wool for the smaller pillows. **Opposite bottom right:** In this kind of an open plan, Mr. Mount feels it is important to have a kitchen that looks good from anywhere. Cabinets, outlined in white oak, are covered in the same gray lacquer Formica as those in the rest of the room; countertops throughout are black marble. **Left:** A trio of pedestals and dramatic lighting turned a small, nondescript hallway into an important-looking gallery for art.

JAMES LEVIN

DINING SPACES

Today's life-styles seem to make the dining room the most expendable room in the house. Builders often eliminate it completely in new construction, and people who do have a dining room would often rather convert it to something more "useful," such as a den or an office. But we all have times when nothing but a "formal" spot will do for entertaining family, friends, or business associates. A possible way to create one is to study other spaces (foyer, den, bedrooms) and see if they might work for dining, too. In this section, you will find a wide range of potential locations, plus space-making ideas for small dining rooms as well.

A Double-Duty Hallway

When designer Lorraine Cook found her floor-through apartment in a New York brownstone, she was struck by its highly stylized wide central hallway. The work of Ben Benedict and Carl Pucci of the architectural firm Bumpzoid, its ziggurat-like walls had been sheathed in glass and chrome to echo the facade of the Empire State Building. The result was a space that provides not only a dramatic entrance to the apartment, but also a fine foil for Mrs. Cook's classic 18th-century Hepplewhite dining-room furniture.

Opposite top: At most times, Mrs. Cook uses the space as an entrance foyer and the furniture is set in place ornamentally. Notice how the walls, as they narrow at the rear of the space, bring the eye the full length of the room to focus on the garden entrance. **Opposite bottom:** When Mrs. Cook has formal dinner parties, the table is easily opened and the chairs pulled up. The glass-covered walls make the light shimmer and bounce, opening up the space and magically softening the boundaries so the eye's not sure where things really end. In this room with many angles, the glass provides a much more subtle and interesting effect than would have come from mirror. The clear plastic chandelier, designed for the room, is another tribute to the Empire State Building.

A Book-Lined Library

The owners wanted a library as well as a warm, inviting dining room for company meals; what the house offered was a dining area with a picture window looking into an added-on enclosed porch. Designer Robert K. Lewis solved the problem simply, by covering over the window and creating a dramatic dual-purpose room within. The now-windowless wall (at rear in photo) gives the room a large focal point as it sets off ever-changing pieces of American folk art.

Left: A large stripped-oak table, a 19th-century copy of a 17th-century Flemish-style banqueting table, commands the center of the room. Closed, it functions as a reference and reading table; extended for dining, it seats 10 (eight Windsor chairs are brought in from the family dining area in the kitchen).

JAMES LEVIN

Hideaway Dining Tables for Unlikely Spaces

Located in an apartment wing used by three teenage sisters, the room below gets its normal workout as the girls' own living room and exercise room. But when their parents have dinners that call for a space more formal than that used for family meals, this room does a real turnaround. The secret lies in three circular tabletops that were created by Carey Clark, an artist. Working with the room's designer, James Ruddock, Miss Clark painted three acrylic rounds, two of which are hung, when not in use, over fiberglass light shields; the third sits on a low wooden base and is used as a coffee table. When it's time for a dinner party, the three tops are placed on folding wooden bases and folding chairs brought out from the closet. Everything in its place, the room seats 18.

PETER LOPPACHER

Dinner is a movable feast when you have a beautiful table that can be used in many parts of the house. For clients who like to give large dinner parties, Bob Patino and Vincente Wolf designed two pairs of wooden forms that can supplement the seating in their dining room. Assembled, the two-part tables can be used in the hallway, above, and in several parts of the living room. Off duty, they're stored in a hallway closet.

Opposite top left: Because the girls use this as an exercise room as well as a sitting room (a bicycle for working out is kept at the opposite end), furniture is minimal and easily movable. The upholstered chairs open out flat for lounging; cabinets under the double window are outfitted for audio equipment (fabric-paneled end cabinets house speakers). Window seats flanking the fireplace flip open for extra storage. **Opposite top right:** Mr. Ruddock removes one of the pieces of acrylic artwork from its light shield, which is sculpted in a similar motif. "The permanent sculpture relief solved the problem of what would be on the wall when the tables were being used." **Opposite bottom left:** One hall closet holds the three folding X-shaped wooden table bases, 18 chairs, and the table linens. **Opposite bottom right:** To give the room a gentle, romantic light that would set the mood for dining, Mr. Ruddock installed a cove ceiling around the perimeter of the room, illuminated from behind by a single row of long, narrow light bulbs. Deep, mirrored window reveals bring in the glittering city skyline. Like the window shades, the chairs' seats and backs are made of taffeta.

A Collection-Filled Foyer

Designer Mario Buatta is an inveterate collector—of objects, botanical prints, dog portraits, fine furniture, and, among his favorites, blue-and-white porcelain and beautiful books. He finds them near home and on his many travels, remembering always the details of each discovery. Because he enjoys being surrounded by them, he has assembled the porcelain in a place of prominence: the octagonal entrance foyer to his apartment, where guests and clients are received. Books are stacked informally on table and chairs, each inviting exploration and enjoyment (below).

Because the kitchen is nearby (door at rear), this is the room he chooses to use also for dining. The Staffordshire, Delft, and Chinese Export porcelain make the room and table setting not only beautiful, but intensely personal as well. The octagonal table, skirted to the floor in red silk, echoes the shape of the room; the set of armchairs, upholstered in leather, once belonged to the late fashion designer Norman Norell.

PETER LOPPACHER

An Off-Center Table Opens a Room

There's no rule that says a dining table has to go in the center of the room. By setting it to one side in this 1950s suburban New York house, designer Robert K. Lewis opened up the room—and the view to prize-winning rosebushes and a tennis court beyond—and gave it visual interest that distracts the eye from the actual size of the room.

The starting point for decorating was a recess in the wall that in earlier times would have been used to set off a fine buffet. Mr. Lewis used it instead as a cocoon for a freestanding banquette on one side of the table. Located as it is near a wall, the table enjoys a warm, sheltered feeling that befits small dinner parties. For larger groups, the table can be moved to the center of the room, leaves added, and extra chairs brought in. Recessed lighting was strategically placed so that both locations have proper down-lighting that operates independently.

JAMES LEVIN

A Scaled-Down Table Fools the Eye

Here's a spatial illusion where the scale of the furniture performs the magic. This oval table, especially when used in combination with Mies chairs, immediately makes us think of the more monumental ones used in much larger modern homes, and in substantial offices as well. But for this 7-by-8-foot dining space, designer Joseph Lembo has scaled it down to 27 inches wide by 84 inches long. It seats just four or six, but its presence is much greater.

JAMES LEVIN

A Flexible Dining Room and Library

Don't always take a room at its face value. A spacious dining room, for example, may have met the needs of a family who lived in a home 50 years ago, but it could be a real space-waster for a family living there today. Such was the case here. Today's owners are a young professional couple with a small child. And although they like to entertain graciously, they had little need for a dining room devoted solely to serving 20 at a time. What they did want, however, and found the apartment lacking, was a library where they could read, listen to music, and watch television, a place that could be used as comfortably by the immediate family as by friends. The plan that designer Mariette Himes Gomez devised fills all their needs, and more than doubles the usefulness of the room.

Above: Today this is a much-used room because it's the family's spot for reading, listening to music, watching television (TV is opposite the right banquette), having meals alone. **Opposite top:** For entertaining, the round 19th-century French table in the foreground can be expanded with three leaves to seat 10, and the 19th-century Regency dropleaf table in front of the banquettes can seat four. Chairs are also 19th-century. **Opposite bottom left, center, right:** An 18th-century French piece has been outfitted for glassware, liquor, stereo components, and television. Shelves, drawers, and the television's pull-out shelf were carefully built and installed so that they can be removed without damage to the antique piece.

A Family Room That Converts to a Dining Room

One problem modern apartments often present is boxy rooms that seem to be inflexible: A living room is a living room; a formal dining room, a dining room. But with a young son and daughter and an impending divorce, the woman who lives here felt she wanted fresh-looking spaces that would adapt better to her family's needs. Their bedrooms would serve as private spaces for sleeping and watching television, and it was important to have a communal place where the three of them could re-lax, play, talk, do homework, and have family meals.

Designer Kevin Walz's solution was to transform the 13-by-17½-foot dining room into a hardworking family space that could be converted, when necessary, into a more formal dining room for guests. The key is the furniture: a luxurious-looking seating banquette of durable materials, three small tables on casters, a serving counter, and three stacking chairs.

RAEANNE GIOVANNI

Opposite: When the space is set up as a family room, two of the three marble-topped tables are stationed under the counter at left; the third parallels the seating unit. Because it is 29 inches high, the children can do homework, play, or have meals here. The seating unit, which is freestanding so that it can be moved to other parts of the apartment, was designed by Mr. Walz to take a lot of hard wear. The back is made of Masonite and covered in galvanized steel; the cushions are leather filled with down.

A pass-through in the wall behind the seating allows easy conversation, as well as serving, from the kitchen to the family area. It also makes the family room feel less confined because it acts as a window by catching the views in the kitchen window beyond. **Above:** As a dining room, the space comfortably seats six when the three 24-by-40-inch tables are lined up at the banquette and the stacking chairs are in place. The serving counter was designed to take spills and heat—it's made of the same material as garbage cans, galvanized steel.

PETER LOPPACHER

An Office for Dining

The most compatible uses for multipurpose rooms are those that don't infringe upon one another, such as working at home and having dinner parties. The former we do when we're alone; the latter, when we have guests.

Equipped with a generous table that serves as a partners' desk plus plenty of easily accessible bookshelves and storage, the room opposite was created by architect Carl Hribar as a study for Rosette Arons and her husband, Alvin Schechter, both designers, when they work at home.

But when a dinner party is planned with more guests than the nearby dining room seats, the table is called into action to handle four more as is, or can be pulled into the center of the room to seat six or eight. Dinner at their desk, they've discovered, is fun for guests, and can be a nice change of pace for family meals, too.

SLEEPING SPACES

It's not just overnight guests that seem to be a logistical problem these days (though, of course, they are). But where should we put ourselves? If we have a studio apartment, do we want to have a bed right out in the open? Or do we want to hide it away and pretend we have a real living room? If we have a bedroom, is that the best use for it? Or would it make a nice home office, or a library? In which case, where do we sleep? And the guests. Always the guests. The living room? The den? Could they really sleep in the hallway? The options are endless.

A Living Room Where Parents Sleep

When baby makes three—and the apartment has only one bedroom—some rearranging is definitely in order. "It seemed particularly important to my wife that our child have a room of her own," says Richard Trask, who lives here with his wife, Jean. The decision they reached when Kimberly was born was deceptively simple: She would get the bedroom, while her parents would move into the living room.

In deciding how to sleep there, the Trasks evaluated the alternatives. A sleep sofa, they determined, would be a nuisance to use every day; a Murphy-type flip-up bed would eat up 2 feet of valuable wall space, and they would still require a sofa. So they opted for the queen-size bed they had, and Mr. Trask designed the furniture they needed around it.

JAMES LEVIN

Opposite: In its usual guise, the bed acts as a sofa. Covered pillows lean against a Parsons-tablelike buffet, under which the bed fits. **Above top:** With its newly installed wheels, the bed can easily be pulled out and uncovered for sleeping. A shelf in the buffet, hidden most of the time by the pillows, can be used for night-time necessities. **Above bottom:** Because the bed's buffet unit extends into the room 2 feet, Mr. Trask decided to minimize its impact by designing a series of wall units that are based on the same 2-foot depth. This module, planned to make the mismatched audio components look built in, supplies space for music, liquor, even stacks of shirts. The matte-white finish is the result of more ingenuity: Because the estimate for lacquering was prohibitive, Mr. Trask trailered all the unfinished furniture to a garage that spray-paints, among other things, Rolls-Royces and sculpture for a prominent artist. The cost was a fraction of what lacquering would have been.

The Library Is a Guest Room

A full-time guest room is becoming a rare commodity these days, not only because space is so costly, but because our personal interests are putting demands on the spaces we have as well. If you're lucky enough to have an "extra" room, you could, of course, reserve it for guests who use it only part-time. But you could also devote it to a more pressing need, such as an efficient place to work at home, perhaps, or an inviting spot to read and write, and still include an overnight guest in the plans.

When Joy and Robert K. Lewis moved into their 1830 house in Cold Spring Harbor, New York, they decided to use this main-floor room for guests and furnished it with an antique daybed and a comfortable chair. It was not long before they craved a place to sit and read, and Bob, an interior designer, added bookshelves from floor to ceiling. Now this is a much-used room where the couple can read—one curled up in a chair, the other stretched out on the daybed—and, when needed, there's still a place for guests.

The Office Is a Guest Room

Designer Laura Bohn planned her own loft with a floor plan that would be wide open except for one thing: She wanted her office, where she works full-time, to be clearly separate so it would be quieter and so that she could "go home" at night and leave her work behind. That made it a perfect choice to use as a guest room. One wall has bookshelves and a long work surface; the other, a mat-covered platform (with storage inside) that doubles as a sofa for clients and a bed for guests.

JAMES LEVIN

Centering a Bed Creates a Separate Dressing Area

Here's a standard bedroom in a typical high-rise that has more storage and style than you might have thought possible. It's the result of eliminating the obvious—a bed on one windowless wall, a bureau or two on the opposite—and seeing the possibilities of every inch. By raising a large area of the floor and placing the bed in the center of the room, designer Mark Epstein was able to make the skyline the focal point. The clients got a view, plus a perfect place to build in an easy-to-watch television set and extra storage. And the change in levels also broke the room into two distinct areas, so that the bureau that serves as a headboard defines a separate dressing area—a nice luxury today—that is adjacent to the bathroom.

Below: The custom bureau has drawers facing the lower-level dressing area and curved doors on the ends. Built in are reading lights and, at the far end of the top, a panel that holds a telephone and controls lights, television, and stereo (speakers are built in over the closets).

JAMES LEVIN

120

Tiny Bedrooms That Double as Studies

Tiny bedrooms present problems in any event, but the dilemma is compounded when the space is to accommodate other functions. The two rooms here, both of which belong to single career women, are used for sleeping, but they're just as important to their occupants as den/studies where they can read, write, watch television, or work when they're home alone.

JAMES LEVIN

Below: Once the territory of two side-by-side Colonial-style beds that ate up most of the floor space, this bedroom, which belongs to Marion Gibbons, was given a sleek new look by designer Bruce Bierman, who began by angling sofa-like sleeping facilities into a corner to open the room. The mattresses came from the old beds; the platforms, slightly higher than conventional bed frames to take advantage of a river view, have a total of four storage drawers. Now there's room for a comfortable upholstered chair with reading light, and the wall behind the chair (not visible) has a long counter incorporating desk and file drawers. Vertical blinds along the wall at right transformed a broken-up window wall into a space-stretching continuous surface.   **Right:** The key to the success of this stylish little room is the way the bed was incorporated into the built-ins so not an inch was wasted. The foot abuts a carpeted counter used as writing desk, vanity, and television table (the open space below the television can be used to store large items such as suitcases), there are storage drawers in the bed's base, and the bureau acts as a headboard. With the bureau situated as it is opposite the closet, which has space-saving curtains instead of doors, the bedroom has a convenient dressing area. Designed by Keller Donovan for Paula Rice Jackson, a magazine editor.

PETER LOPPACHER

A Living Room with Bed-Size Sofas

Here's a living room where two sofas can do nighttime duty because they're as wide as twin beds and have single arms that make fine "headboards" for someone who likes to read or watch television in bed. When she decorated this one-bedroom apartment for a Florida resident who uses it as a New York pied-à-terre, Sybil Levin chose these sofas because they would provide sleeping space for the client's grown children when they spent the night. The stripped pine armoire has plenty of drawers for overnight clothing storage, and hides the television when not in use, too.

JAMES LEVIN

122

A Small-Scale Sitting Room for Sleeping

"Bedrooms should all be sitting rooms," says Lemeau of Lemeau & Llana, who designed this room. "You should be able to do everything in one room—sleep, read, eat, get made up and dressed." How do you do that in a room that measures 9 by 12 feet? The answer here was built-ins. "I don't believe in bureaus unless one has enormous space. With built-ins you can go right to the ceiling or the picture moldings." Here she added two units: bookshelves behind the bed and, though she had only 14 inches of depth with which to work, a 44-inch-wide closet that turned a wasted corner into a tiny dressing room, complete with vanity and adjustable pigeonholes for wardrobe, personal appliances, and magazines.

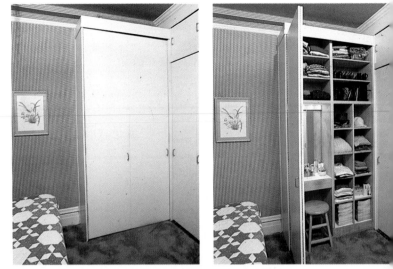

JAMES LEVIN

Built-ins for a Closetless Bedroom

If you have more clothes than your bedroom has closet space, consider the advantages of built-ins: They can utilize every inch of wall space right up to the ceiling, no matter what shape it is, and can be sized exactly for what they're going to hold, so that no space is wasted.

Before a wall of storage was built, this room, part of a much-expanded log hunting lodge, had no closets at all. Designer Beverly Ellsley, who lives here with her husband, Bob, took advantage of the wall where the room's door was located, had it fitted out with drawers and cupboards, and then flaunted their contents. All whimsically hand-stenciled and -labeled (by Mrs. Ellsley), these built-ins now have all the cachet of a vintage haberdashery. They also give the room a strong focal point and make it feel more spacious by incorporating the doorway and exaggerating the ceiling height.

JAMES LEVIN

A Full-Size Bed in a 6-Foot-Wide Room

The facts were irrefutable: A bed is 6½ feet long; the room was 6 feet wide with no chance of expansion because the wall backed onto an elevator shaft. What to do?

Dexter Design placed the bed with its side to the wall and turned the room's long, skinny shape into a design asset. Headboard and footboard are spacious storage units; with a closet near each of the units, husband and wife have separate dressing areas. So the bed wouldn't feel as if it were in a well between the storage units, it was raised on a platform, which also maximizes the view. A slanted mirror overhead softens the room's corridorlike shape, magnifies the light, and brings in the view when the owners are in bed.

JAMES LEVIN

An Angled Wall Expands a Bedroom

Much of the feeling we have about a particular space—whether it is cozy or cold, expansive or cramped—comes not from its actual size but from how we experience it. This bedroom, in designers Bob Patino and Vicente Wolf's own apartment, for example, feels open and airy. Yet the room measures only 11½ feet wide at the windowed end by 18 feet long, and the ceiling is a standard height. What gives it the illusion of greater spaciousness is a combination of three things: a white-on-white color scheme; a spare design; and, most of all, the use of angles. By turning the right-hand wall 45 degrees off its straight course (and echoing the line with the bed), the designers created a forced perspective, so the space seems longer and wider than it is. The translucent glass inset permits light to pass through and makes the wall seem less solid, and therefore less constricting.

PETER LOPPACHER

127

A Sliding Screen Creates a Bedroom

With its alcove extension, an L-shaped studio has a lot to offer. Don't think of the extra area as merely a place to tuck a bed so it's out of the living room. Think of it instead as a study, an office, a place to devise an exciting sleeping arrangement, perhaps another room entirely. With proper planning, that "bonus" space can fill any one of a variety of needs while keeping your total living space to a manageable minimum.

The man who lives here asked designer Eric Bernard for a scheme that would allow him to utilize the whole space when not entertaining, and to enjoy the flexibility of having his bedroom either exposed or closed off when he had guests. The solution came in the guise of shoji-inspired screens and extensive built-ins that are as carefully planned as those on a yacht.

Opposite top and bottom: Three sliding panels with adjustable louvers are on a wall-to-wall track and can close off the bedroom entirely, permit a partial view, or, left wide open, allow the apartment to be used as a whole. A change in floor levels and surfaces, from the hardness of tile to the softness of carpet, was used to give the bedroom area a sense of presentation. Lights under the bed lessen its great mass and make it look as if it's floating. **Right top:** Sound equipment is located so that it can be used easily from either the bedroom or the living room. **Right bottom:** The television, which can be operated from the bed, is on a pullout shelf and swivels so that it is visible from the bedroom or from the living room. The floor-level panel to the right of the desk is a built-in file drawer.

A Little Jewel Box for Sleeping

If you long for the elegance of a formally decorated bedroom, don't feel you need a room of monumental proportions. This room by Zajac & Callahan measures a mere 11 by 12 feet, but everything about it is absolutely splendid. The key in a small space, says Richard Callahan, is using a very few rich and luxurious furnishings, and then showing them off against a background where all surfaces—walls, ceiling, floor—are the same color. "It makes the room like a little jewel box, a rare case where too much of a good thing is better."

JAMES LEVIN

Above: A richly patterned chintz, the same color as the carpet, was used to drape the ceiling and to upholster the walls, which are hung with good-quality Hogarth prints. Furniture includes a Syrie Maugham bed and two Louis XVI chairs. Room designed for the Kips Bay Show House.

Sleeping Niches

Nothing could be cozier than a sleeping niche, a place where curtains or cupboards surround a bed and turn it into a wonderfully warm and charming private world. In small spaces, however, a sleeping niche often does much more: It can give a small room a surprising amount of architectural interest, and it can even create a room within a room, thereby making the space appear larger than it is.

Below: Picture this teenager's room with an ordinary single bed wedged between entry and closet doors—that makes it easy to see what a difference a cupboard bed can make. Says designer Beverly Ellsley, "I wanted this boring little rectangular space to have as much stature as the rest of the house." By using the cupboard bed, Mrs. Ellsley introduced an important-looking architectural element that changed the room's emphasis from horizontal to vertical and added storage in the base as well.   **Right:** Would you guess that this space, which looks like a glorious lady's sitting room, is actually a very regularly shaped 10-by-16-foot room? The pretense of having two rooms, which gives the illusion of more space, was accomplished by designer Gary Crain by dividing the room with columns and beam, then treating the halves of the room to different fabrics.   **Far right:** In the front portion of the space, created for the Kips Bay Show House, an elaborate chandelier gives the impression of a grander-size room.

BATHROOMS

Designing a small bathroom that's both functional and good-looking requires real ingenuity but is more feasible than you might imagine. You can find fixtures created both for small spaces (don't overlook those made for boats, trailers, or laboratories, all of which are readily available) and for awkward spaces, such as corners. If you use a tub for bathing as opposed to showering, you don't need much headroom and could install it under eaves or even a staircase. If you want to give your bathroom the illusion of more space, you could install the tub at floor level, or even put it *below* floor level covered by a trapdoor. Look for equipment that serves more than one purpose (a mirror-doored medicine cabinet with built-in lighting, for instance), and consider whether travel-size personal appliances might serve your needs sufficiently. Not only will they take up less space in the bathroom, but they'll also eliminate your need for storing extras.

Two Bathrooms That Share a Tub

Building a separate guest bath in a house can be expensive and space-consuming—and particularly wasteful if it's not going to get a lot of use. It is nice, however, to be able to give guests some privacy and maintain the privacy of the master bath as well.

The bathroom shown here does both by striking a clever compromise: The tub area was designed to be shared by owners and guests, both of whom have their own sinks and toilets. Here's how it works: The owners have a 5-by-6-foot bathroom that's sep-arated from the 6-by-6-foot tub area by a pocket door; most of the time, the door remains open and the entire space is used by the owners. On the other side is a 3-by-6-foot room for the guests' sink and toilet, with access to the tub area through a conventional door. Either door can be locked when the tub area is being used. The result: two bathrooms in the space of one and a half. It was designed by architect Carl Hribar.

James Levin

Above: This part of the bathroom is entered from the upstairs hallway. Mr. Lewis moved the new sink out in front of the plumbing and thereby made the counter ample enough to display some of the family's prized pottery.   **Opposite:** This section of the bathroom is reached through the Lewises' dressing room. Because of the eaves, this sink was moved out to gain adequate headroom. The toilet (not visible) is to its right.

Two Bathrooms That Share a Shower

Houses built before indoor plumbing was invented have unique sets of problems when it comes to bathrooms. The 1830 house of Joy and Robert K. Lewis had one upstairs bathroom when they bought it, but with two young sons, the Lewises wanted another.

The existing bathroom was long and skinny, with eaves that cut down on some of the available headroom. What Mr. Lewis did was design a bathroom for each end of the space and, right in the middle, put in a stall shower that is accessible from both sides through doors whose glass is translucent for privacy.

Using Mirror for Impact

Mirror is one of the best friends a small space can have: It can lighten and brighten, widen a room or lengthen it, add dimension, even make boundaries disappear. But one thing that must be kept in mind, in any room, is what the mirror reflects. A busy room looks at least twice as busy when it's reflected in a mirror, and no one is enthralled by images of mechanical ducts or plumbing, something that deserves particular attention in a bathroom.

Below: This small, handsome bathroom is in the heart of a high-rise and had no view, so Patino/Wolf used large expanses of mirror to create one. Sitting above a surface of white tiles, the mirror makes the boundaries "disappear" and puts the focus on multiple views of elegant fittings.   **Opposite:** In designer Laura Bohn's own home, mirror reflects one of the highlights of her loft: a 5-foot-round soaking tub, which is actually a horse trough treated to a coat of deep aqua epoxy paint.

PETER LOPPACHER

JAMES LEVIN

Opening Up Old Bathrooms with Mirror and Light

Here are two bathrooms with very different beginnings (one is in an old apartment building, the other in a tract house) that were opened up and given great style by the addition of light and mirror.

Opposite: A true Cinderella transformation, this was once a plain little bathroom in a tract house. Designer Joan Halperin closed off an unattractive window, added a skylight instead, and used lots of mirror to reflect the light. Although it's a very small bathroom, there's

plenty of storage—a hamper and cabinet under the sink, four drawers, and two medicine cabinets (not visible). **Below left:** A wonderful mix of old and new, this white-tiled bathroom retains its vintage fixtures but has had its fittings, from lighting to shower track, brought up to date. Designer Kevin Walz mirrored the top section on one whole wall and added two recessed mirrored medicine cabinets. With lighting suspended in front, it has all the polished gleam of the silver accessories on the shelf. **Below right:** Chrome pegs line the wall facing the mirror end to end in photo below, holding towels and acting as a strong design element.

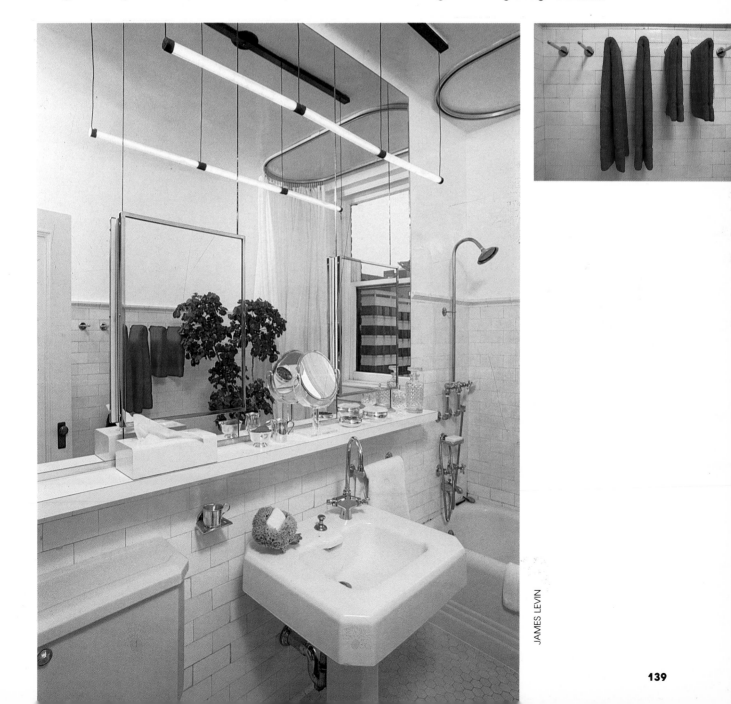

JAMES LEVIN

Trompe l'Oeil Adds Dimension

For centuries, decorative painters have been practicing the art of trompe l'oeil to make us perceive something that doesn't exist. In the case of this bathroom, which is in a stone house that resembles a Tuscan villa, interior designer Beverly Ellsley asked Neil and Sue Connell to transform the bathroom into a grotto complete with fountain, a feat they accomplished with paintbrushes.

But even more than just enjoying this artful deception, there are lessons to be learned from these trompe l'oeil tricks: The texture and depth of the stones and the sculpture in the niche add dimension to the walls, and the monochromatic gray coloring expands the sense of space.

JAMES LEVIN

Special Problem-Solvers

Of all the small spaces that tap our ingenuity, bathrooms are probably at the top of the list. There are givens to deal with (location of plumbing or windows, for example), as well as needs (proper light for putting on makeup or shaving, a place for tissues or magazines). Here are some good problem-solvers.

Left top: In this tiny bathroom, every inch was put to work. Dexter Design added a drawer over the toilet, installed a magazine rack in the side of the vanity, and recessed a tissue box in the wall below the medicine chest. **Left bottom:** There are sinks available to meet almost any space requirement, many of the odd ones (small rounds, for example) produced for commercial and industrial use. In the angled corner of this bathroom, designer Kevin Walz used a stainless-steel rectangular sink with hospital-type faucets in a base of white cabinets. **Below:** The best place for the sink was not on a wall but under the window, so Kevin Walz located it there—and installed the necessary mirror on an arm. No space is wasted, and the mirror is bathed in natural light.

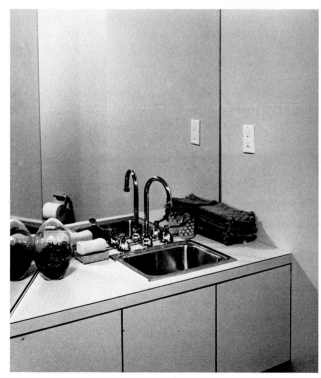

JAMES LEVIN

MEDIA SPACES

It had to happen. Just as audio components were getting smaller and even the most-cramped-for-space listeners could delight in stacking a whole system into one little bookcase (and, if the TV didn't fit anywhere in the house, it could be strapped to the wrist), along came the big-screen TV, truly a problem of gigantic proportions. But few of us would give up our pleasures of sight and sound, be they big-screen TV, big-sound stereo, or mountains of reading material, just because we were tight on space. Here's how to deal with them.

A TV Room within a Living Room

When a couple is home alone, it's nice to have a comfortable place to watch television and enjoy a quiet dinner. This intimate spot is just that, yet it's part of a much larger wide-open living room.

The key is the floor-to-ceiling media unit, which

Patino/Wolf designed to shelter the space while allowing access around both sides to the living room behind it. The coffee table, which they also designed, spins up to dining-table height.

A Small Room Decked Out for Media Equipment

The best way to enjoy electronic equipment to the fullest is to devote an entire room to it. This one measures only 10 by 14 feet, yet because of the clever seating—two loveseats plus four ottomans that slide into the walls—there's room for eight people to enjoy the electronics.

Marc Klein of Marc Klein Interiors covered over the room's three windows, then built two oak cabinets to house all the elements. On one wall (below left), from the top: Dahlquist speaker; Nakamichi cassette player; Mitsubishi vertical turntable; Sumo amplifier, preamplifier, and tuner; plus storage space for cassettes and records. On the other wall (below right), from the top: Dahlquist speaker; two Teknika component television systems with screens set below their tuners; a JVC video machine; and an Atari home computer. The bright green lighting in the soffit and in the room's entryway was inspired by video games. Room designed for the Kips Bay Show House.

A Dining Room That Incorporates a Den

Like most Americans, the family of four who live here spend more time watching television and visiting together than having formal dinners. So they asked designer Richard Mervis to take what would traditionally have been the apartment's dining room (the door at rear leads to the kitchen) and give them a space that would function as a family den as well as a formal dining room.

By arranging the furniture with the dining table at the far end, closer to the living room, Mr. Mervis was able to include an L-shaped seating arrangement. The unit of cabinetry he built against an existing wall houses a television and videocassette recorder and also stores china and serves as a buffet counter. Lit from above and mirrored on the back, the cabinet wall is so "open" it almost looks like a pass-through.

JAMES LEVIN

Room for a Big-Screen TV

To set a large-screen television into a room of any size is a task that is somewhat tricky. There are, first of all, technical requirements: the optimum location of the screen; whether or not the room has to be darkened for the particular set; and, if it is a two-part system (separate screen and projector), placing the components at the prescribed distance apart, plus making sure there is no traffic pattern between them. Then there are decorative considerations such as how prominent the television should be and how furniture can be arranged for the best viewing.

In the room shown here, designer Rubén de Saavedra has expertly dealt with the requirements of the modern technology without detracting from the splendor of the turn-of-the-century space. Deep cabinets surround the screen to minimize the impact of its depth, and the coffee table incorporating the projector is stainless steel because its reflective surface makes it seem less bulky.

Pivoting Bookshelves Expand Space

These shelves do more than hold books: They make the library/guest room below feel more spacious because they turned what was once a chopped-up wall with two doors into one continuous surface. The surprise is that the doors are still here, concealed by portions of the bookcase that swing open to allow access to a bathroom and to a closet for guests, for whom the banquettes can be made up as beds. The bookshelves have an additional purpose as well: They give the space a sense of color, texture, and a three-dimensional feeling. Designed by Melvin Dwork.

RALPH BOGERTMAN

Above left: Mounted on custom-made heavy-duty pivot hinges, the two doors swing out to allow access to the bathroom and, to the left of the clock, the guest closet (not shown). **Above right:** On the felt-covered wall perpendicular to the shelves, flush doors open to reveal a television.

A Media Retreat

A retreat devoted to reading and writing, listening to music, and watching television was what designers Bob Patino and Vicente Wolf had in mind when they created this room in their apartment. An elevated platform stacked with pillows gives them a place to relax, much as if they were sitting on the floor, and incorporates controls for television and stereo in the back, as well as a telephone in the base. A cabinet opposite the platform (bottom) unites television, stereo equipment, and shelves for records, tapes, and books.

PETER LOPPACHER

148

A Hallway Becomes a TV Room

The parents wanted a place for the children to watch television, but not in their rooms. Taking advantage of the spacious hallway leading to the family bedrooms (doors are seen closed here), architect Carl Hribar installed a banquette and recessed a television in the wall opposite.

Book Nook

Just big enough for a loveseat and two walls of floor-to-ceiling bookshelves, this space gives designer Lorraine Cook a private place to read or have a quiet dinner on a tray. A star-pattern quilt adds warmth to the brick wall; a Lucite coffee table "disappears" in the small space.

WORK SPACES

Having the proper place to work at home, whether it's dealing with office paperwork, paying bills, sewing a dress, or pursuing a woodworking hobby, can make any task more pleasurable. It isn't always necessary to have a lot of work space. And where it is located doesn't necessarily matter, either. You could steal a corner from kitchen or den, hide an office in a foyer closet, create a dual-purpose space for dining and sewing, perhaps. What counts is having a place set aside that's convenient and organized.

An Office/Dining Room

When the book editor who lives here found her three-room apartment, it had an oddly shaped, viewless center room that didn't seem to have any purpose. But she lacked a dining room, and needed, too, an at-home office and a place to enjoy her dressmaking hobby.

Designer Lemeau of Lemeau & Llana devised a plan that would accommodate all three, one at a time. Traces of working at home disappear when the many-sided console desk unfolds to become a library dining table and a pair of Windsor chairs are pulled alongside; fabrics for sewing are stored inside the banquettes. A closet (not shown) holds a computer and other work supplies.

JAMES LEVIN

150

A Bedroom/Study

A home with a study may sound ideal, but not, necessarily, when the household has *two* adults who frequently work at home. "My husband monopolized the study, and I needed a place to concentrate, read, and work at home as well," says Susan Lewin. "What I had was an ordinary master bedroom—and no place to put anything."

The Lewins called in Michael Haskins, an interior designer, who incorporated everything Mrs. Lewin needed into the room, so now it is her private haven as well as the master bedroom. There's a chaise, a vanity, and a place for her books right where she likes them—near the bed. "Since college I've had the habit of working in bed," she says. The shelving design was a collaboration: Mr. Haskins proposed a grid of shelves for books and supplies; Mrs. Lewin, who is creative director of Formica, suggested her firm's Color Grid coordinated laminates for the backs. The work table, also surfaced in Formica, is on wheels and is kept over the foot of the bed when not being used.

PETER LOPPACHER

A Desk in the Bathroom

The office at left was created by designer Ann Le-Coney for her husband, Michael, when "quite literally, we ran out of space." Although the LeConeys' home is large, new additions (three children, a housekeeper) changed their priorities, and Mr. Le-Coney's succession of offices kept getting taken away from him.

So when he wanted a small and cozy place where he could open mail and go over reports without having to worry about how neat everything looked, they decided on a corner of one of the master bedroom's two bathrooms. With a stall shower, adjacent toilet, and a small sink vanity, there was a wall free for a long desk, which is mirrored behind; shelves reach to the ceiling.

JAMES LEVIN

An Artist's Studio in the Den

Because its windows fill it with wonderful daylight, the room below became the obvious choice for a studio when the apartment's owner married an artist. But he had used it as a den, and they felt they needed a guest room as well. Now it can serve all three functions, thanks to designer Kevin Walz's addition of a work table where she can paint and a shelf just wide enough to hold canvases. The leather Anfibio sofa unfolds into a full-size bed.

A Bed/Desk Unit

When wall space is limited because of doors and windows, constructing a freestanding bed and desk unit can be a terrific problem-solver. Laura Bohn designed the one below with walls that define and contain each area and covered all the surfaces in the same beige carpet as the floor so as not to break up the small space. And because the walls are carpeted, they make a good surface for hanging pictures on the bed side, tacking up memos on the desk side.

JAMES LEVIN

An Office in a Closet

Here's an "office" (right) that can hold endless clutter, but it can all disappear because it's in a closet. It was designed by the owners for their bedroom because they wanted to keep the small room as neat as possible. Although the closet measures only 3 by 4 feet, it has about 45 running feet of shelving, plus room for versatile sliding baskets. The closet door makes a perfect place for a folding shelf for paying bills or using a portable typewriter.

All of the components of this office in a closet are readily available throughout the country: Vinyl-coated steel shelves and basket system are Closet Maid by Clairson International; the 1-inch-wide step stool used to reach the top shelves is from Black & Decker; the folding plastic shelf is by Syroco. A closet conversion like this lends itself as well to sewing, ironing (a board could go on the door), small woodworking projects, or painting.

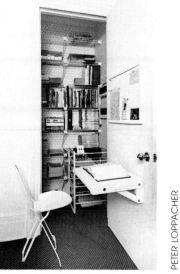

PETER LOPPACHER

KITCHENS

In the early 1900s, Bernard Maybeck, a noted American architect, hung an oven on a wall and installed a stove in a counter, and ever since then we have been striving to utilize our kitchen space to its fullest. Although we rarely go to the extremes of the Europeans, who have mastered small-space kitchens with cooktops that flip up against the wall when not in use and tiny refrigerators and freezers that are stacked in a wall or slid under counters, we have learned to cope by using specialized storage, scaled-down equipment, multipurpose appliances (a stove/oven/dishwasher in one, for instance), and even dishes that do double-duty for cooking and serving. And what we've learned in the process is that a small kitchen can be very efficient—and, yes, even desirable.

But for many of us, a spacious kitchen with room to cook, have family meals, and visit with friends is the ultimate. In this case, we're fortunate if we can add on; but it's also possible to "expand" by stealing some space from adjacent rooms.

In this section, we take a look at both types of kitchens: those that deal successfully with the confines of tight spaces, and those that have been able to break out and grow.

JAMES LEVIN

Little Kitchens with Style

The room at right is a before-and-after story that started with a small, neglected, 60-year-old kitchen with a refrigerator as its focal point. Because his kitchen is the first thing you see when you enter the apartment (this photograph was taken from the front hall), designer Tom O'Toole gave it a major facelift, updating the floor plan and dressing the room up with color and shine.

Stealing space from the unneeded maid's room behind the kitchen, Mr. O'Toole first stretched the 8-foot-wide space to 17 feet in length, and then tucked the offending refrigerator away with its back to the wall adjacent to the entry door, so it isn't seen immediately. The wall and ceiling you do see glitter with space-expanding mirror, a wash of light from the cove ceiling, and a splash of bright red glossy paint chosen "because it's a boring little space."

Instead of using upper cabinets that can close in a narrow room, Mr. O'Toole opted for open shelves with concealed lighting over the work counter and a wall of pantry closets opposite (not shown). The 19th-century French pastry table can be used for food preparation and for unloading the dishwasher. The rear of the space, the former maid's room, has a counter lit by two hanging fixtures that's designed for having breakfast or doing paperwork.

PETER LOPPACHER

Located in an old building whose apartments, over the years, had evolved into strange, cut-up spaces, the small, irregularly shaped room opposite had been allotted to the kitchen.

To get the best use of what space was available, architect Alan Buchsbaum gutted the room and started from scratch to give the client both good storage and a place to eat. New upper cabinets are double height so there's no wasted space above, and a triangular table wedged between window and counter makes room for breakfast for two, studying recipes, or extra work space. Under a window is a particularly good place for a counter because a heat source is often there, making the space useless for appliances or cabinets.

A Kitchen Expanded for Family Living

Sizable houses built many years ago often had relatively small kitchens intended to be used only by servants. Like the other small rooms for household help, they were relegated to the rear of the house and were designed to be nothing more than functional. Today, however, the family is just as likely to be handling the cooking, and the kitchen is often the center of a household's activities.

With four active children and a yard and pool that were inaccessible from the kitchen, the family who live in this 25-year-old house felt their antiquated kitchen setup needed a major overhaul. They wanted a big room that would accommodate the children and their frequent guests, without having them in the way when someone was cooking, and one that would be easy to reach from the yard and pool. Designer Robert K. Lewis began by gutting the entire area from the dining room to the garage: Walls came down between the old kitchen, breakfast room, laundry, rear hall to the garage, and back stairs, yielding one wide-open room that measures 16 feet wide by 50 feet long. Then two sets of French doors replaced existing windows and a deck was added outside them to connect the whole space with a porch as well as the yard.

Opposite top: Although this room is large, the actual work space was kept tight to make it as functional as possible. Appliances are in the ideal triangle pattern: sink in the island counter, stoves (one gas, one electric) on the rear wall, refrigerator on the wall perpendicular (not visible). Open shelves, which make it easy to reach tableware, are a good space-stretcher in any size kitchen because they maximize the full length of the room, instead of visually cutting it a foot or so short as cabinet doors would do. **Opposite bottom left:** French doors lead to the back yard for easy access to the pool; the paneled door in background at right opens to the garage. The far wall, painted the dark green of the other accents in this white kitchen, hides new back stairs to the bedroom floor, where the laundry has been relocated. The centrally positioned table and sink island permit an easy flow of foot traffic. The under-counter opening to the left of the sink is for a trash basket. **Opposite bottom right:** Because the children enter from the garage door and often use the rear stairs to reach their rooms, it was important to have a place for them to stash their coats and gear. So Mr. Lewis devised this freestanding unit that has cubbies facing the door and creates a corridor connecting to the back stairs; its other side is an upholstered seat for the dining table.

Right: The wall facing the French doors is a spine of full-height storage that reaches the entire length of the space and incorporates refrigerator, ice machine, a desk, and a coat closet, as well as pantry storage. All are accessible without going into the actual work space of the kitchen. The buffet in the foreground is storage and a serving surface for the dining room and is topped with Corian so that hot or cold foods can be put directly on it. The oak floor, added to tie all the spaces together, is laid on a diagonal, a good way to make any rectangular space appear wider.

Storing It All

Having enough storage is a problem in any small space, but nowhere does it seem more pressing than in the kitchen, where everything should be right at hand. If you're starting a kitchen from scratch, either building or remodeling, there are a number of manufacturers who offer complete cabinet systems that are outfitted with pantries, pull-out racks and bins, built-in step stools, even small breakfast tables that pull out from under the countertop. If you're planning a custom kitchen, don't overlook any small space; many condiments, for instance, don't require much room and could fit into recesses built between a wall's framework. And, in any kitchen, you can take advantage of today's abundance of ready-made storage accessories, such as wall grids, stacking baskets, ceiling-hung pot racks, and shelves that will maximize your use of existing cabinet space.

A compact two-cart garage houses an entire *batterie de cuisine* within a loft designed by Kevin Walz for fashion designer Adri, thanks to readily available wire storage accessories. Pots, pans, and tools hang on hooks from grids; cookbooks are conveniently stored on shelves; and the carts, one with a chopping-block top, can be rolled out for working.

In the kitchen, a cupboard doesn't have to be very big. Most spice jars, for instance, are only about 4 inches high and fit into a small space such as this.

JAMES LEVIN

Don't overlook any niches. In designer Larry Shattuck's kitchen, a series of inexpensive wire racks holds a cupboardful of dishes and serving pieces. On the floor below there's room for liquor bottles and a basket of magazines.

A niche above the sink in this renovated brownstone apartment is a handy place for spices. It's also a reminder of bygone days, when this was the top of a fireplace opening.

Here's where cutting corners makes sense. The angled cabinet in designer Laura Bohn's kitchen has been put to good use with two shelves for staples.

A charming wooden rack holds and displays plates in just inches of space in this kitchen eating area designed by Richard Neas. This piece is one of a kind, but it's an idea that could easily be borrowed.

Three Small Rooms Yield a Spacious Kitchen

What started as a 12-by-12½-foot kitchen is now an expansive space that measures 20 by 29 feet, complete with family dining area, pantry, and work space for four or more, thanks to Charles Mount's reworking of the suburban house's former kitchen, furnace room, laundry, and staircase.

Below: At the kitchen's center is an all-in-one work island and dining table of Paradiso marble with a honed finish. With two Jenn-Air ranges (marble sides are raised around them to contain any spatter) set into a long counter, several cooks can easily work at the same time, and the children can watch television because it's behind the black doors set under the stairs, which formerly made a 180-degree turn into the room. An oval stainless-steel structure overhead incorporates lighting and pot rack. **Opposite top:** Near the refrigerator in the rear of the photograph is a separate baking area with counter and ovens. The cabinets here, as in the major work space in the foreground, are hunter green laminate with a shiny lacquer finish (New Design Concepts by Formica), trimmed in natural oak; countertops are white Corian. At the rear of the room, glass block encloses a new pantry and lets light pass through to the kitchen from its two existing windows; at night, track lighting in the pantry supplies the glow. A ledge on the kitchen side is sized for cookbooks. **Opposite bottom:** French doors were substituted for existing windows, so now there is direct access from the kitchen to the porch.

JAMES LEVIN

A Small Kitchen Becomes a Great Room

Whether you call it a heart-of-the-house room or a great room, one space that integrates kitchen, family dining area, and den has much appeal for families who live informally. It's also a great visual space maker because one large room always feels more spacious than equal square footage broken into two or three separate rooms.

This space got its start as a kitchen, located right where it is now, and grew into a warm, comfortable heart-of-the-house family room with a clever addition made from an old barn.

Left: Designer Beverly Ellsley created the room by knocking down the existing kitchen's exterior wall, relocating its cabinets, and attaching an addition the same width as the old kitchen. The new room was constructed from one bay of a small barn, its structural beams cut down, remortised, and rejoined. The beams in the kitchen, also from the barn, are decorative, added to tie the two spaces together as one. **Below:** Fitted storage makes the best possible use of wall space, since there are no "wasted" areas as there would be around freestanding furniture. These cabinets comprise two window seats, base cabinets for television and stereo, and shelves that hold books, collections, and serving pieces used for dining.

JAMES LEVIN

Three Ways to Deal with Tight Spaces

Many a spectacular meal has been prepared in a minuscule kitchen. The secret, any good cook will tell you, is being organized and efficient. A lot of space is not necessarily a big help. In fact, many good cooks prefer a small kitchen, where everything is only a step or an arm's length away. In spaces such as these, however, it is vitally important to take note of details: to make sure that refrigerator and cupboard doors open in the right directions; that there is adequate access to dishwasher and oven; that you have a place to put down food and pots next to the refrigerator, range, and oven.

On these pages are three good-looking, efficient kitchens that clearly illustrate that there's more than one way to treat a small space. One is a spare, minimal design; another owes its look to ships' galleys; and the third thumbs its nose at today's conventional wisdom of paring down small spaces and is a delightful cornucopia of objects and patterns.

JAMES LEVIN

Above left and center: By the time the stove, sink, and refrigerator were installed in this tiny kitchen, you might have thought there wouldn't be room for much else. But designer Mario Buatta has a full complement of cabinets and still has room for the porcelain he collects. Making expert use of all the wall space between counter and upper cabinets, a simple shelf and a wire rack add a second level of storage for dishes and even a small television. Plates attached on wire holders to the faces of the high, little-used cabinets are not only pretty to look at but emphasize the ceiling height

as well. Because they're only 24 inches deep, Sub-Zero refrigerators such as this are a good choice for tight spaces.   **Above right:** Most typical of all small kitchens is the galley plan, a corridor with facing rows of cabinets and appliances. It is a workable, step-saving plan that ideally has sink and stove, separated by a work surface, located on the same wall. Dexter Design planned this kitchen with plastic-laminate-covered storage right up to the ceiling and then gave it an expansive feeling by eliminating detracting hardware and coloring it all a bright, light-reflecting white.

Opposite right: Sheathed in wood, this tiny kitchen has the look; and the efficiency, of a well-planned ship's galley. To keep the room from having a tunnel shape, owner/designer Larry Laslo "shortened" the room by using doors to close off two of the shelves on the rear wall and "widened" it with mirror behind the sink counter. Shelves don't waste an inch; they were designed to be just the right heights for their contents. **Opposite left top:** By boxing in the space around the

stove (the refrigerator is next to the wall at right), Mr. Laslo was able to outfit this space as precisely as a cabinet: The right wall is now usable for storing knives, and the dish/pot rack makes good use of the void above the stove.   **Opposite left bottom:** Because the kitchen is so small, a table was placed right outside the door. It can be used as an extra work surface or, as it is here, for setting out a buffet. Linens are stored in the decorative box and basket under the table.

CHILDREN'S SPACES

Children have problems that are uniquely their own: playthings that are messy and games that are often noisy; heights that make "normal" furniture and bathroom fixtures difficult to use; a need for open floor space where they can play. Their visual senses delight in the colorful and the fanciful, and, perhaps even more than adults, they crave privacy and spaces of their own. For all these reasons, and many more, we have devoted a separate section to making space for children.

Pint-Size Storage

A three-and-a-half-year-old loves searching for his special toys, dressing himself, setting tables for make-believe parties—all things that are difficult to do if he can't reach or find what he needs. So Joan Halperin designed everything in the room below at just the right height for the young man who lives there.

Toys are kept in a system of gray-painted wooden modules that are lined up so he can reach everything; as he grows taller, they can be stacked higher.

Red plastic bins on the shelves keep all the bits and pieces together. A few inches inside the closet Miss Halperin built one step that he can climb so he's only an arm's length away from his clothes and toys, all kept on wire shelves. But he found another use for it as well: He loves to sit on the carpeted step and pretend he's in a special little house. His tot-size table is a wire spool, painted black and fitted with a black Formica top.

PETER LOPPACHER

A Castle for Sleeping and Playing

When it comes to having a spot to sleep and play, what could make any young girl happier than a castle of her own?

Beverly Ellsley designed the one below for her own daughter, Rebecca, in the space of a single bed. There's a hideaway inside (where she can also stash toys at night), bookshelves on the side facing the windows (not shown), and a ladder on the other end for climbing up to her bed. The only other things in the bedroom are a closet and a long shelf with chair, which she can use as a desk.

JAMES LEVIN

A Room Divided Horizontally for Two Children

Two into one will go—even if the two children are different ages or sexes and the size of the one room seems impossible. Here and on page 170 are ways to make space for siblings in very typical bedrooms. Because this room is about twice as long as it is wide, the best solution was to divide it on the horizontal. The seven-year-old girl has the half by the windows, her three-year-old brother the portion by the entrance door, and the storage unit that separates their spaces stops short of the ceiling to let light and air filter through. A pocket door can be pulled across the accessway to give them privacy. The design is by Richard Mervis.

Below: The boy's space has room for a twin-size bed, bureau, closet, shelves for toys and books, and a desk for him to grow into. Mirroring behind the shelves at left magnifies the light (important because there are no windows) and makes the wall "disappear" and the space feel twice as wide.   **Opposite top left and right:** The girl's space has a closet with an Elfa system of pull-out baskets for clothes, plus two hanging rods.

Opposite center left and right: A long desk and bookshelves fit neatly around the window. Two storage drawers under the bed were built with heavy-duty drawer guides on the sides, wheels below. Carpet was carried over the bed platform to keep the floor surface continuous, thereby making the area more spacious in feeling.

JAMES LEVIN

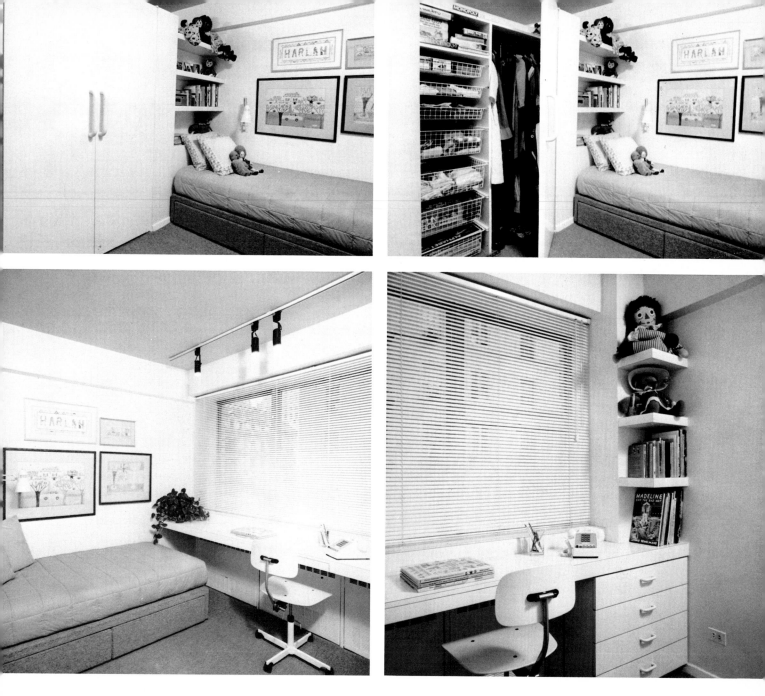

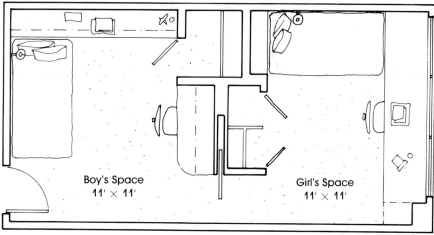

Boy's Space
11' × 11'

Girl's Space
11' × 11'

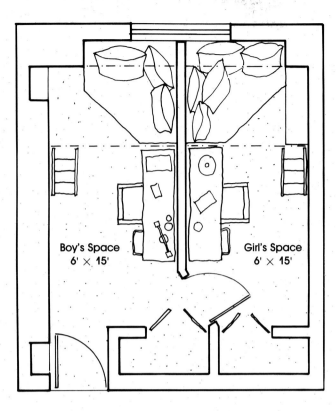

Boy's Space
6' × 15'

Girl's Space
6' × 15'

A Room Divided Vertically

The givens were these: two children—a daughter, 14, and a son, 13—and one bedroom, measuring 12 by 15 feet with an 8-foot ceiling. The room had only one window, one closet, and an entry door in one corner. Their mother, an interior designer whose professional name is Toni Spottswood, set out to solve the problem by constructing a clever dividing wall of 1-inch-thick acoustical panels. It starts about a foot out from the central window, so both children get light and air, and slices across the room before angling into the off-center closet (see plan). The result is two spaces whose furniture arrangements are mirror images. Each child has a loft bed, sofa, and desk, plus half a closet outfitted with rods and shelves that utilize every inch. Miss Spottswood and a friend did all the work themselves, from constructing the wall and furniture to laying the carpet.

Below left and right: Because the children needed only enough height for sitting on their sofas and beds, Miss Spottswood was able to "stack" the furniture. There are 3½ feet of headroom over each bed and 4 feet over the sofas, which are wedges of cotton-batting-wrapped foam covered in sturdy movers' pads. Their ends fit precisely against the ends of the desks. Colors were limited to gray and beige with touches of black so that the small space wouldn't look broken up, as it would have with highly contrasting colors.

RALPH BOGERTMAN

A Jungle Gym of a Room for Two

This is a room for sharing—and for playing. Its occupants are two boys, ages four and five, with two beds that hug one wall end to end (a dividing partition at their feet has round holes for peeping), a loft that houses side-by-side desks, a floor space left open for playing, a sofa for watching television, and a wealth of places to hide, climb, and stash treasures away. It was planned by their mother, designer Ann LeConey, with Lemeau of Lemeau & Llana, who took advantage of the 13-by-18-foot room's high ceiling to get two levels of activity on each of the four walls and maximum open floor space at the same time.

Below: Because headroom is unnecessary for sleeping, the beds are tucked under a 47-inch-high ceiling (with airplanes painted overhead) and the desk loft above has full standing height. Every possible inch around the beds was put to good use: Each boy has a little shelf for a flashlight, built-in lights, drawers under his bed, storage closets recessed into the walls. Over the sofa there's a ladder built for climbing and swinging.

Above left and right: All the boys have to do is climb a step at the left end of their desk loft and they're in a wonderful tunnel with peepholes that stretches over their built-in bookshelves and bureaus. Along the wall perpendicular (not visible), the tunnel has railings instead of peepholes as it crosses over two back-to-back closets with a climbing ladder on the side of the closets facing into the room. A stowaway table has two folding front legs and two rear hooks so that it can be slipped over a rung on the ladder.

JAMES LEVIN

Room for a Teenage Boy

Many apartments, especially older ones, have small maid's chambers that, if not used for domestic help, are adaptable to any number of needs: office, nursery, guest room, storage. Today, with city living space particularly tight, many parents are turning to them as bedrooms for older children.

The space below, designed by Kevin Walz, began as a very typical maid's room: It had room for little more than a bed and, in a space-saving move, incorporated a sink so that only the toilet and shower had to be included in a separate bathroom. When Mr. Walz was called in to transform it into a stylish room for a teenage boy, he decided to take advantage of the room's austere beginnings and turn them into a design asset. Now an Italian sink and faucets, left, decorate the pale gray wall like a piece of sculpture, and the sleek plane of mirror above is actually a medicine cabinet. Bookshelves and a built-in desktop maximize the irregular space around the window and provide a convenient ledge behind the bed, which has storage drawers in its base.

JAMES LEVIN

Room for a Teenage Girl

Located in a brownstone, this teenage girl's room typically measures a scant 7 by 11 feet, but her requests were many: a sophisticated bedroom where a friend could stay, a desk and vanity, book storage, and a grown-up dressing area with plenty of mirrors.

Designer Richard Mervis included them all by breaking the room into three areas (see plan): A desk/vanity got the choice spot, under the window with a view of a park; a sleeping area has a twin-size bed with a trundle bed below and lift-up storage for linen behind it; and a dressing area was created by clothing cabinets in the side of the bed unit facing a whole wall of mirror, which incorporates the closet. "People are often afraid to break up small spaces," says Mr. Mervis, "but it really gives the illusion of having more space."

Another device that abets this deception is the use of angles that aren't quite 90 degrees. They create interest in the room and help obliterate its boundaries.

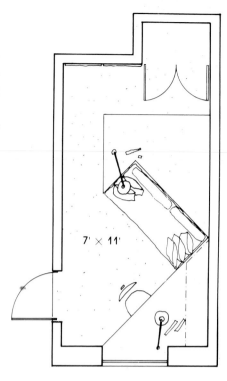

7' × 11'

A Disappearing Playroom

Finding a place for children to play with their toys is always difficult in an apartment, especially when it's a sleek, minimally designed one. But John Saladino solved the problem ingeniously for one family by creating this dual-purpose room that's for playing by day and dining by night. The secret is hidden behind two closed doors—one a triangular cabinet behind the sofa (note how the mirror expands the piece and makes it look like a large square), the other a closet located to its right.

Opposite: When it's time to play, the dining table rolls off to one side and the wide-open wooden floor has room for a tent and chairs, which are stored inside the triangular cabinet; the half-circle table is attached to the door. The closet holds toys and games, and it's lined in cork for showing off artwork.   **Below:** In its normal guise, the room has both a table for dining and a seating area with sofa, chairs, and table raised on a platform to take advantage of the view—perfect for drinks before dinner or coffee after. For larger dinner parties, the oval table on the platform can be set there, or divided in half and added to the ends of the rectangular table.

FOUND SPACES

Take a thoughtful look around your house or apartment. Is the space above the refrigerator in your kitchen being wasted? What about installing a hanging pot rack or a couple of shelves there? Does your den have a table topped by a beautiful skirt, with nothing but unused space beneath it? It could be just the spot for a file cabinet, a stack of magazines you want to save, or even a small refrigerator. Could you turn a bedroom closet into a real dressing room? Or put a small makeup table under that sunny window? All of these are what we call found spaces—existing areas just waiting to be discovered. Here and on the next five pages are a range of imaginative ideas to start you thinking.

RALPH BOGERTMAN

PETER LOPPACHER

Above left: An extra seating spot. There's room in the foyer when the sofa snuggles into the curve of a dramatic staircase. By Dexter Design.

Above right: Room for a piano. Patino/Wolf created it in a hallway of an apartment with a wide closet. Recessed lights overhead, a mirrored back wall, and a painting make it a glamorous setting for a white piano.

Opposite: A spacious dressing table. It's a shelf only as wide as the column it abuts at right, but four side-by-side drawers hold all that is necessary. By Kevin Walz.

A library, a home office. Mariette Himes Gomez found space in what could have been just a decorative corner of a large multifunctional room, right. The table, an oversize adaptation of a Shaker candle-stand, can be a reading desk, conference table, even an extra dining table.

JAMES LEVIN

A delightful dressing room. In this 7-by-11-foot space, Ir-vine and Fleming concocted a comfort-filled room they call "a little candy box." Mitered Regency-striped pa-per tents the ceiling, and a curious child, painted on mirror, peeks in to watch her parents. The bar is a painted tin tray; the sofa, a tiny Chippendale settee—a piece that's very useful in a small dressing room such as this, at the end of a bed, in a small hallway, or un-der a window.

JAMES LEVIN

A quiet spot to read or write. It's nothing more than a simple chair pulled up to a dressing-room window to take advantage of the view of rolling lawn and peren-nial gardens. In the home of Joy and Robert K. Lewis.

A light-washed dressing table. Architect Carl Hribar carved it out of a corner between window and built-in clothing storage, for coauthor Lois Perschetz.

A record library. Shelves in this hallway go floor to ceiling to hold records and music scores. By Rubén de Saavedra.

A vanishing workshop. Wire grids hold tools and other necessities in a closet that's only inches deep. In the home of Rosette and Alvin Schechter.

Space for books. Shallow bookshelves in a hallway hold hundreds in this apartment by Dexter Design.

Space for a foyer "table." A conventional table would have crowded the entry, so Dexter Design substituted an angular wall-hung shelf with two drawers.

A bedroom desk. Square edges would have looked cumbersome, so Richard Mervis used a spacesaving curved door that hides shelves.

Desk with a view. A wooden shelf
stretching across an oversize window is ample space for writer David Fisher's typewriter. By Carl Hribar.

SPACE MAKERS

When it comes to shaping existing space, or creating usable space where there was none, there are certain structural and decorative devices that are so useful they warrant special attention. Therefore, they are gathered here under the title "Space Makers." Most of them appear elsewhere in the book as solutions to specific problems, but here you will see them highlighted on their own so that you can study them and see if they will help you create the particular space you need.

Mirroring, a Partial Wall

Mirror is a spectacular space maker. Used on the short wall of a narrow room, it makes the room look deeper; used on the long wall, it makes it look wider. It can lighten a room, add dimension, even make a solid wall "disappear," as it does in this living room. By mirroring the wall at the end of the banquette, Dexter Design opened up the room *and* the skyline view, which seems to go on forever.

The new curved wall solved the problem of a bathroom that opened directly off the living room. The partial wall provides a sense of separation, but because it stops short of the ceiling, it doesn't close off the living room and make it smaller. More space makers here: *glossy paint* to push back the walls, bounce the light around; *minimal furniture*; *a built-in banquette* to get the most seating in the space (carpeting on the base creates a *continuous floor surface*).

JAMES LEVIN

A Semi-Wall, Pivoting Panels

One of the best ways to give a room the illusion of more space is to "borrow" visually from another. A living room, for example, will feel more spacious if your eye is able to go beyond the living-room boundary and take in the dining room or kitchen as well. Here are some space makers that allow you to do just that, while at the same time defining a sense of separation between the areas.

Opposite: This dining room is part of a larger continuous space that includes a living room, a long entrance hallway, and a staircase, in the home of coauthor Lois Perschetz and her husband, Arthur. But architect Carl Hribar has defined each element while maintaining the maximum openness. Three panels pivot on hinges top and bottom to divide dining room from hallway and stairs. Set on an angle, they open the view and add architectural interest; wide open, they accommodate large-crowd traffic; closed, they make the dining area more intimate. More space makers: A *dropped ceiling* and *exaggerated column* to further define the dining area within the larger space; *pipe railings* on the staircase instead of a closed-in railing.   **Below:** A semi-wall—a partial wall that is high enough to give the spaces it divides a feeling of separation but low enough to maintain an expansive feeling—is particularly well suited to informal living situations. For clients who wanted their kitchen, but not the mess, open to the dining area, designer Bruce Bierman devised a wall that, at 48 inches, is a foot higher than the work counter sheltered behind it. The semi-wall hides the counters and appliances (on a center island and back wall) from view, and, with a cutting board built into one end of its counter, serves as a perfect spot for a bartender to dispense drinks at a party.

BRUCE BIERMAN

Greenhouses

One of the simplest, and often the least expensive, ways to get additional space is to build a greenhouse. It can enclose an outdoor area such as a terrace or patio so the space can be used full-time, or can be attached to a house to create a new room entirely, a particularly wonderful idea for a home spa, family room, or dining room.

JAMES LEVIN

The top floor of this small duplex penthouse consisted of a 16-by-16-foot living/dining room with a terrace and a small kitchen. By enclosing the terrace with a greenhouse, Dexter Design created an additional multipurpose room that's sun-filled work space by day, star-roofed dining space at night.

LORD AND BURNHAM

In this country house, a Lord and Burnham greenhouse was set atop a second-story balcony to give the owners a sky-high living space that allows them to enjoy the view of their property all year round.

JAMES LEVIN

In this apartment by Dexter Design, a sheltered banquette with its back to the entry was built to extend the living-room seating. The side facing the front door (not shown) is a backdrop for a foyer table.

Space-Defining Units

Many newly built apartments and houses are plagued by the problem of disappearing spaces. Entrance foyers, bedroom hallways, dining rooms—all have been eaten into (and often completely taken away) by rising building costs. In many cases, front doors now open directly into living rooms, so there is no longer a spot that serves as transition from street to home, a place to greet guests, or perhaps have them remove their coats before confronting others in the living room.

One favorite solution of interior designers is to use a freestanding unit that in essence separates the entry and living room. Those shown here are custom-designed, but you could also use a ready-made unit. A piece located as these are makes space two ways: It creates a foyer on one side, and it "enlarges" the living room on the other by having usable furniture at its extremity. It's also a good way to add extra storage.

This unit, sheathed in stainless steel, was designed for storage by Richard Mervis. Its curved ends open to reveal sound equipment and records, the side facing the entry (not shown) has shelves for books, and the center section facing the living room is outfitted as a bar. Note how the bar's mirrored back and glass shelves give the illusion that the interior is open.

JAMES LEVIN

The Artful Use of Color

Dark colors make walls recede; light colors make them expand. Applying both decorating devices, designer Robert K. Lewis created a dramatic telescopic effect in this bedroom. He did it by exaggerating the room's three ceiling heights. The lowest height, encompassing the entrance and closets, was most constricted, so he painted it the darkest to make it appear even more so. Next is the bed area, painted slightly lighter. And the window area, where the ceiling is highest, was painted the palest shade to really open it up. The three bands of color are repeated in the carpet. Panels of pleated unlined silk at the bed's corners emphasize the height of the room, as does the row of vertically hung classical engravings.

JAMES LEVIN

Paint to Fool the Eye

With billowing clouds and distant mountain peaks glimpsed beyond a trellised surround, this charming breakfast corner captures the open-air feeling of dining on a terrace. But its magical qualities belie its location—the far end of a rectangular kitchen, once partitioned off for storage—and the fact that the space has no windows. Decorator Mario Buatta suggested the theme to decorative painter Robert Jackson, whose trompe l'oeil is so light-filled and captivating that visitors to the kitchen find themselves gazing "outdoors."

PETER LOPPACHER

As the rooms on the previous pages clearly illustrate, there is more to making space than just skillful design and decorating. In many instances it's the products employed that give a room multiple uses, or that allow you to fit more than you would have thought possible into the space you have.

In this section you will find a wide range of items that can help. To give them some sense of form, they have been arranged loosely by their usual functions, but, of course, where they would actually be used depends on your personal situation. (A freestanding coat closet, for instance, is included with living-room furniture, though you may be looking for one for your bedroom or home office.)

Instead of including tried-and-true, easy-to-find products such as small-scale stereo components, stacking storage baskets, and folding metal chairs, we have concentrated on more unusual ones.

Many of the items you will see are true classics, proof that they have stood the test of time and an indication that they will be readily available throughout the country. Other items are newer, and, though we assume they will be obtainable at the date of this book's publication, the ultimate decision rests, naturally, with the manufacturer. Prices, similarly, are subject to change, but we felt it important to include them as a guideline.

Addresses for resources are in the directory on page 219. Each is followed by a symbol: (M) for manufacturer or distributor; (R) for retail store; (T) for to the trade only, through architects and designers; (MO) for mail order. For items indicated (M), contact the manufacturer or distributor for the retail source closest to you.

Many manufacturers, of course, make similar products (camelback sleep sofas and stacking washer/dryers, for instance), so you can use this product directory not only as an actual shopping guide, but also as a source of ideas to get you started looking for your own selections.

As we all become increasingly aware of the space crunch, manufacturers of residential products are turning out more and more items from which you will be able to choose. Keep in mind, too, that contract furnishings (those for large-scale applications such as hotels and restaurants) are often suited to saving space. Though generally more expensive than similar items intended for residential applications (because they are geared to heavier use), they are well designed and well made and may not be available through residential outlets. Good sources for these are the *Sweet's Catalogue File* used by professionals (and available in libraries) and your telephone book's Yellow Pages.

FOUR MAKING-SPACE PRODUCTS

PETER LOPPACHER

1

2

3

4

5

(1) A settee by architect Michael Graves is small and graceful enough for the tightest of spaces. Royal blue velvet upholstery; ebony-inlaid bird's-eye maple frame, from Sunar. $4,609.   **(2)** In canvas or linen with a polypropylene frame, this easy-sitting folding armchair from Beylerian can be used indoors or out. $440.   **(3)** Wall-mounted lamps save floor/table space and keep small rooms from looking cluttered. Hansen's Swing-Arm Wall Lamp, in brass or chrome with various shades, is a favorite with decorators. About $180.   **(4)** Everything for

entertaining—sink, storage, refrigerator/freezer, and ice-maker—is together in this 57-inch-long unit from Dwyer. Use it in a family room, behind a bar, against a pass-through wall. In black porcelain (other colors available) with a white Corian top. $2,600.   **(5)** The extra closet you need: a freestanding unit with one contoured door that rotates by means of a touch latch. Intrex makes it in 14 colors and five woods and can add casters for mobility. From $1,645.   **(6)** An artistic solution to not enough seating is this work by artist Tom Loeser, avail-

6

7

8

9

able through the Gallery at Workbench—an interesting addition to a room whether it's hanging on the wall or opened as a chair. By special order. **(7)** Gerd Lange's award-winning stacking Nova chair is used in airports and universities, but it's elegant enough to be used at home. Lightweight but very sturdy, it's available in five colors of molded polypropylene on a steel frame. From Atelier International. $84. **(8)** A classic Charles Rennie Mackintosh chair with a surprise inside: The upholstered seat hides storage below. In ebony-stained oak, it's

called the Willow 1 and is 37 inches wide, 15³/₄ inches deep, and 46³/₄ inches high. From Atelier International. $5,210. **(9)** Storage units make the most of a limited space. This white lacquered one, the Star from Workbench, is a system you can style yourself—cabinets in several sizes, doors, shelves, and drawers are available (38 items in all), priced from $30 to $300.

10

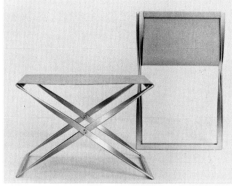

11

14

12

13

15

(10) With today's smaller rooms in mind, Hickory Chair has developed a group of 18th-Century-styled, scaled-down pieces. This Sheraton chair, adapted from a Massachusetts sofa, circa 1800–1810, features a curved-top armpost and lighter wood burl inlay on the arm supports that are characteristic of Boston craftsmanship. From $590. **(11)** Extra seating when you need it: a folding chrome-plated steel stool with seat of oxhide, $1,020, or canvas, $720. Designed by Poul Kjaerholm, distributed by Design Selections International. **(12)** Small in scale, this graceful chair called Villa Galli was designed by Josef Hoffmann in 1913. The upholstery is plush mohair; the legs, ebonized wood. From ICF, $2,400. **(13)** Kittinger's mahogany spider table can hold a lamp or flowers when set against a wall, then be opened when needed for games or light meals. It's 27³/₄ inches high; 29 inches long; 13 inches wide closed, 25⁵/₈ inches open. $1,680. **(14)** It's called the Ciarly Bar, and it's a portable serving and refrigerated storage unit that would be a treat in living room, den, or bedroom. Made of expanded polyurethane (white or black), it has three sections: tray, storage shelf, and refrigeration unit/cooler (the bottom divider can be removed to give the entire lower space refrigeration). Size closed: 30³/₄ inches high, 21⁵/₈ inches wide, 21⁵/₈ inches deep, from Hastings Tile & Il Bagno Collections. Designed by Italy's Carlo Urbinati. $1,545. **(15)** Side table or night table, this storage

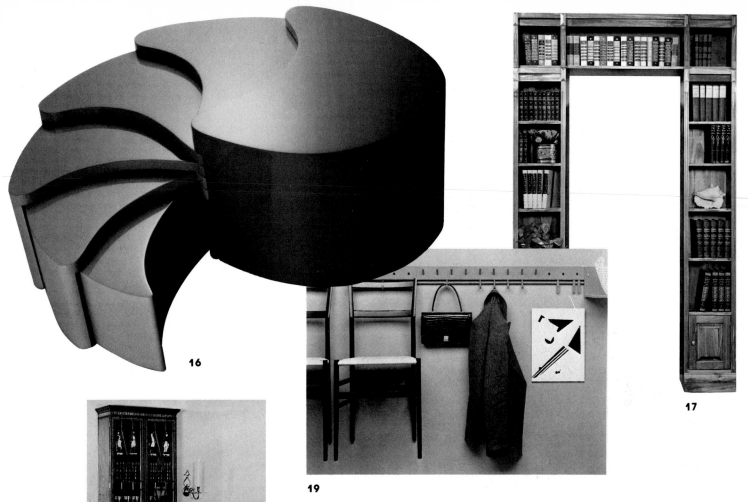

16

17

18

19

20

drum opens with a touch latch to reveal a fixed shelf inside. The Opa Locka Table from Intrex comes in two sizes and 24 finishes. From $975. **(16)** A table of many sizes, depending on how you swing it open, is this Eclipse Coffee Table from Casa Bella, in colored lacquer, brass, or stainless steel. $7,182 in lacquer. **(17)** To take advantage of the unused space around doorways, Curtis has created this three-piece system that combines two side sections and a bridge over the doorway. It comes in many finishes and sizes and can grow with other additions. From $1,000. **(18)** This slimlined mahogany secretary from Kittinger combines three drawers, a desk, and storage shelves into 31 inches of width. $6,720. **(19)** For storage, do as the Shak-

ers did and hang out-of-use items (clothing, extra dining chairs) on a peg rack. This one, however, is not wood but injection-molded foamed high-impact polystyrene of white, red, or gray, with optional shelves and various hooks. The Outline System from Beylerian. Strips are from $28, plus accessories. **(20)** A swing-out table solves many problems. It can be closed in a small space and opened when extra tabletop surface is needed, or it can be kept open in front of a sofa with convertible bed section and closed when the bed is pulled out. Thayer Coggin makes this elliptical shape in bamboo or colored laminate. $633.

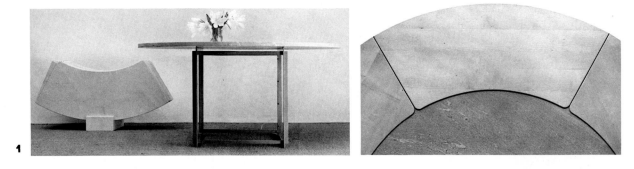

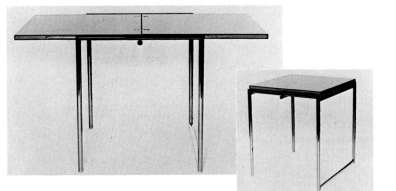

(1) It starts with a 54-inch-round marble top, but this remarkable steel-based dining table by Danish architect Poul Kjaerholm turns into an 82-inch circle with the addition of six leaves of raw maple, which form a ring to encircle it. From Design Selections International. Table, $2,750; leaves, $2,690. **(2)** The legendary Eileen Gray designed this Jean Flip Top Table in 1929. With a chrome-plated tubular-steel frame and maple-edged matte Formica top (black or white), it's 27$\frac{1}{2}$ by 25$\frac{1}{2}$ by 28$\frac{1}{2}$ inches high and opens to 51 inches. From Beylerian. $576. **(3)** A small table such as this one in mahogany veneer from Kittinger, which is 22$\frac{3}{4}$ inches deep when closed, is useful in a living room, library, or bedroom; with the top flipped open to 45$\frac{1}{2}$ inches deep, it can be used for dining. $2,985. **(4)** Here's a delightful folding chair that's as whimsical closed (not shown) as it is open. You can even hang it on a wall. In dazzling colors like red and emerald, it's the Dafne by Thema. Available through Italyca. $59. **(5)** At mealtimes, this teak table measures 34 by 68 inches and has four matching chairs; afterward, the sides fold down, and the chairs fold up and slide into the base, so it can be stored in a small place such as a hallway. From Workbench. $269. **(6)** This extraordinary Maria table, designed by Bruno Mathsson in 1935, is 43$\frac{1}{4}$ inches wide and stretches to a length of 110$\frac{1}{4}$, but it folds

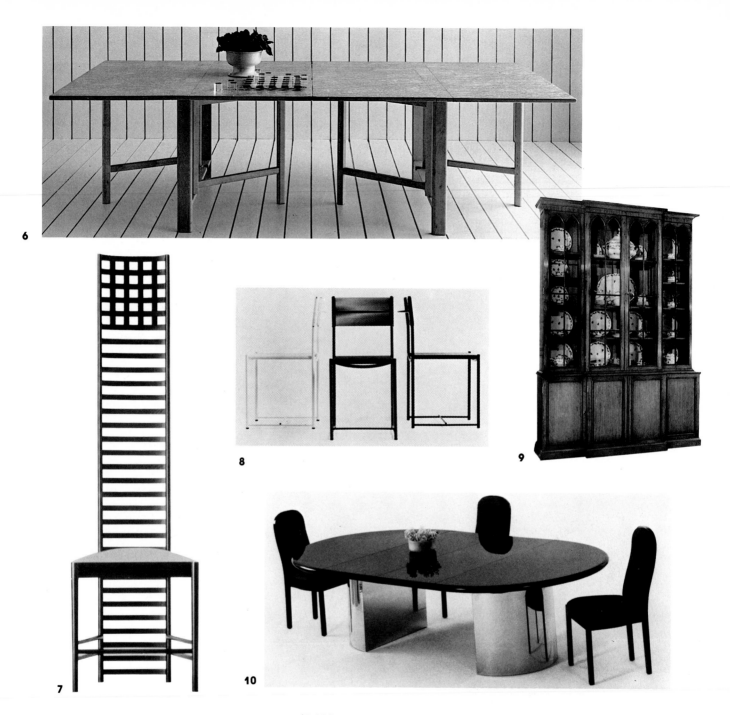

down to 8 inches. Available in natural beech, $2,393, or curly-grained birch, $2,702, from Dux. **(7)** A lot of style in a narrow space: Charles Rennie Mackintosh's Hill House chair, designed in 1902 and made of ebonized wood, is 15³/₄ inches wide and 55⁵/₈ inches tall. From Atelier International. $2,060. **(8)** Spaghetti is the name of this chair, and it measures only 15³/₄ inches wide. But one of the best reasons to use it in a small room is that it's available with clear polyvinyl chloride (PVC) "spaghetti" wound around its steel frame so it's very light in looks. Designed by Giandomenico Belotti and available through ICF. $190. **(9)** If your dining room is short on storage, consider a breakfront for holding and dis-

playing tableware. This one from Kittinger, in mahogany and mahogany veneer, has a traditional face but a streamlined profile: 87¹/₄ inches high, 61³/₄ inches long, 17³/₈ inches deep. $11,915. **(10)** Designed by Paul Mayen, the Toronto Extension Table from Intrex is a handsome lacquer-topped table that's 90 inches long on two half-circles of mirror-polished chrome; when the 18-inch-wide leaves are removed, it becomes a 54-inch circle on a round pedestal (available also in a 45-inch size). $4,122.

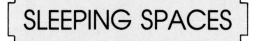

(1) Eileen Gray designed the Lota Sofa in 1929 and it's just as timely today. The mattress and four cushions are available with either down or fiber filling, and the lacquered ends are cabinets that can hold nighttime needs. From Beylerian. $3,865 with down, $2,950 with fiberfill. **(2)** Extra seating/extra sleeping. Thayer Coggin calls it Part Time Ottoman and, with its top cushion re- moved, it pops open into a single bed. From $660. **(3)** A contemporary classic, this injection-molded plastic storage cabinet on casters is handy at bedside or is perfect for double-duty rooms with hidden beds be- cause clock, tissues, and magazines can be stored be- hind the closed door. From Beylerian. $80. **(4)** There's a sofa bed that's suited to every decor. Here it's the

4

5

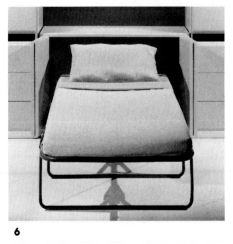

6

classic look of a traditional Chippendale sofa with crewel upholstery and a wood base either 94 inches long with a 74-by-54-inch mattress or 74 inches long with a 74-by-52-inch mattress. By Castro Convertibles. $1,289 and $1,249.   **(5)** For those who favor a futon for sleeping, Arise has developed the Cloud model that has a 2-inch layer of high-compression and high-density foam at the core of its cotton-batting layers. With the addition of two matching bolsters, it doubles as a sofa. $176 as shown.   **(6)** Living room, library, even the dining room can handle an overnight guest when it has a 29-by-73-inch mattress hidden in the credenza. By Thayer Coggin. Bed unit, $895 (other pieces shown, about $475 each).

7

8

9

(7) Firm and luxurious to sit in, this Italian leather sofa called Anfibio unsnaps and opens flat to reveal a sheepskin-covered mattress. From ICF. $5,800. (8) The Lane Company, aware of the growing number of new homes with small spaces, has developed a collection of small-scaled oak furniture called Country Crafts. This storage piece, which is 58 inches wide and 70 inches high, comprises a mirror-doored armoire for hanging clothes, shelves, drawers, and a desklike section. $1,439. (9) Who would ever guess that this good-looking upholstered chair has a single bed inside? Use one or a pair in living room or family room. It's by Thayer Coggin. From $640. (10) An innovator in popular-priced sleep furniture, Sherwood produces a huge

10

11

12

array—about two dozen groupings in 35 fabrics—of chairs, sofas, and chaises that double as beds. Prices range from $99 to $199 for chairs, $199 to $399 for sofas. This grouping is called Tux.   **(11)** Ruffles and skirt give this sofa plenty of outward charm, but deep inside it's a hardworking queen-size bed. The Ashley from Castro Convertibles has a 5-inch-thick mattress and is avail-

able in full size as well. $1,149 for queen-size.   **(12)** This chair turns into a bed, but it doesn't need a pillow, a blanket, or sheets because everything is self-contained: The black cotton foam chair unbuckles; the red-piped black-and-white graphpaper-checked Dacron-filled cover becomes the bedding (it completely zips off to be dry-cleaned). From Workbench. $149.

1

2

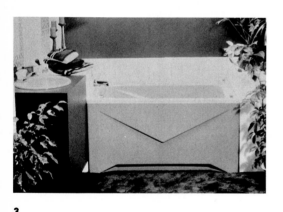

3

4

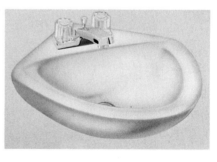

5

(1) By combining compartments for toiletries and grooming aids into one sleek unit, the Lavabo Attrezzato keeps bathroom clutter to a minimum and eliminates the need for extra shelving. The center·section is a mirrored medicine cabinet; the side compartments incorporate AM-FM radio, digital clock, adjustable magnifying mirror, and toothbrush and glass holders; the basin has a hand spray, soap dish, and two towel holders. From Hastings Tile & Il Bagno Collection. $1,880 in white. **(2)** A shower that cuts corners makes the most of tight spaces. The molded-fiberglass Neo-angle model from Lasco comes in 17 colors, measures 18 inches from wall to front angle, 24 inches across the front. $220, without fittings. **(3)** Here's a deep (22 inch-

es) soaking tub that fits into the space of a stall shower. Called The Greek, it's 48 inches long and 32 inches wide and comes in 14 acrylic colors, with optional whirlpool attachments. From Kohler. $406 to $1,300, without fittings. **(4)** A corner toilet is a good choice for a tiny bathroom because it maximizes elbow room. Triangle by Eljer is available with either a round or an elongated bowl, in vitreous china. From $145. **(5)** The Corner Minette, a space-saving vitreous-china sink from American-Standard, is $8^5/_8$ inches from front to back and $12^1/_2$ inches wide. From $132, without fittings. **(6)** Sized to fit through most doorways so that it can be used for remodelings, the fiberglass Bimini stall shower from Kohler is just $32^1/_8$ inches wide and 36 inches from

6

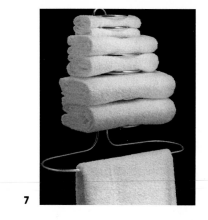

7

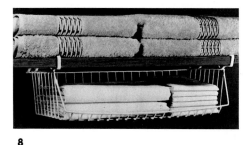

8

9

10

11

front to back. From $426, without fittings. **(7)** The towel holders used by hotels pack a lot of easily accessible towels neatly into a small space. This one from Plaza Towel Holder stacks six and has an optional bar for hanging a damp one. Holder, $7.20; bar, $2.60. **(8)** If far-apart shelves give you wasted space, add a wire rack to put it to good use. Lillian Vernon's is 19¾ by 9¾ by 6 inches high. $5. **(9)** This square shower adapts to any bathroom space because it's 29½ inches wide, but it's a special boon to tight places because it has a see-through wall and door, plus built-in seat and shelves for toiletries. The Antares from Hastings Tile & Il Bagno Collection is made of clear metacrylic and metacrylic-reinforced fiberglass, in seven colors.

With fittings, $1,680 in white, $1,765 in colors. **(10)** In 19⅝ inches of space, this freestanding, rotating column can add an enormous amount of storage. Called the Pipedo, it's equipped with a full-length mirror, two drawers, smoked-glass cabinets with shelves, laundry hamper, robe hooks, and towel bars. From Hastings Tile & Il Bagno Collection. $1,170. **(11)** If you'd like a deep soaking tub, consider the Mikado by Eljer. In fiberglass-reinforced plastic, it has an integral molded seat for soaking or foot bathing, comes with an optional six-jet hydrotherapeutic whirlpool, and measures only 40⅝ by 40⅝ by 34 inches deep. $835 to $2,305, without fittings.

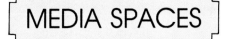

(1) A pull-out swivel shelf holds a television in the top section and shelves below are sized for videocassette recorder and a receiver in the glazed hemp cabinet from Design Institute America. It can be used against a wall, but its size—72 inches wide by 52 inches high by 22 inches deep—makes it a good choice for a free-standing room divider as well. $2,690. **(2)** Pioneer calls its Foresight 7000 system a media room without the room. It incorporates video and audio components (plus record storage) into 6 feet of space. $3,000. **(3)** The Sony Profeel Trinitron Component TV system was developed for its superior "high-fidelity" qualities, but it's also perfect for designing media rooms because the components can be located wherever you want them. Shown here are two monitors, 19- and 25-inch; access tuner; wireless remote control; side-mount

speakers and freestanding speakers; and extension cable. Monitors are $850 and $1,500; speakers, $80 and $130; tuner, $520. **(4)** You don't have to have cabinets made to order to give a big-screen TV a custom look. Thayer Coggin makes a series of cabinets (in many finishes) with a screen canopy and a projector table that incorporates a Sony projection system. Projection table, $675; screen canopy, $343; other pieces shown, from $115 to $580. **(5)** Now you see it . . . but this TV Lift Cabinet is engineered so that the center section and TV disappear into the sleek cabinet. From Devin. $3,848. **(6)** Here's a big-screen projection system that's around only when you need it. Kloss' Novabeam Model Two is a portable projection video monitor (shown here in its "in use" position) that produces a 4-foot, 4-inch color picture on any flat white wall in a

darkened room. The monitor can be wheeled away when not in use, and its design eliminates the cost of an often-redundant TV tuner. $2,200.　**(7)** Another option for big-TV viewing in a small space is the Novabeam Model One Ceiling Mount: The projector is mounted on the ceiling (controls are accessible through a bottom panel); the screen is 10 feet. From Kloss Video. $4,300.　**(8)** Compact discs are not only small (4 inches in diameter) and long-playing (about 60 minutes on a side) but they have a remarkable quality of sound. This Sony compact disc player fits neatly on a shelf and has a linear disc table that glides out of the player, so the unit requires very little space above it. $900.　**(9)** A real boon to music fans with small spaces is a system that spins a record vertically, so the player fits on a narrow shelf and doesn't have

"dead space" overhead as conventional players do. This InterPlay model from Mitsubishi incorporates a metal-tape player. $690.　**(10)** When is a TV not a TV? When it's a radio. Panasonic's double-duty model flips from a vertical digital clock/radio to a horizontal black-and-white TV, making it particularly useful in a bedroom. $210.　**(11)** The Tower from Design Institute America gives you easy access to TV, videocassette recorder, and receiver behind a pair of see-through doors in the top section, hidden storage behind doors below. $3,310.　**(12)** Small enough to keep on a night table or a desk, this color TV from Sony has a 3.7-inch screen that swivels for easy viewing. $580.

WORK SPACES

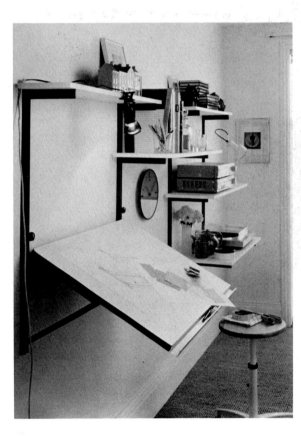

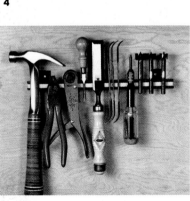

(1) Of all the full-size washers and dryers made today, White-Westinghouse's are the only ones that can be stacked (in 27 inches of floor space) or installed under a kitchen counter (side by side in 54 inches). They have a 14-pound capacity, and the dryer is available in gas or electric. Washer, $630; electric dryer, $370. **(2)** Red plastic caps hook into any perfboard so you can just unscrew the jars and take the contents wherever you need them. Use them for nails and screws in the work-shop, spices in the kitchen, snaps and buttons in the sewing room. From Brookstone. Ten containers, $5.95.

(3) One of the handiest desk/storage systems around is Rakks, composed of black aluminum standards and brackets, white laminate shelves, and an adjustable white drawing board that slides up flush against the wall when not in use. Available at Conran's. Drawing board, $95; standards from $8.95 each; shelves, $3.95 to $18.95. **(4)** Create your own organized ironing area with Rubbermaid's holder for board, iron, spray starch, and other items. $5. **(5)** This 13-inch magnet bar is

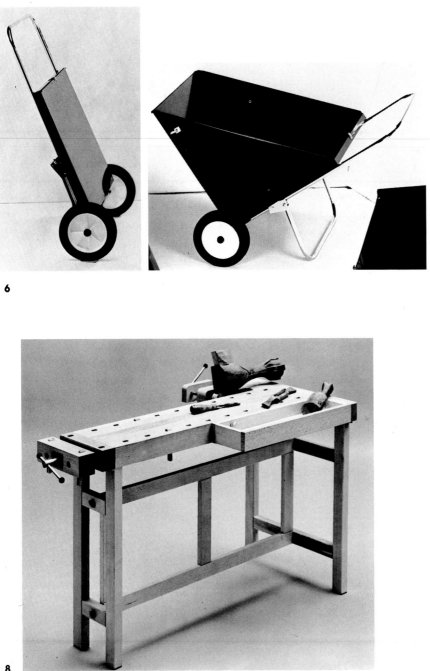

6

7

8

9

strong enough to be crammed with tools, including round ones. From Leichtung. $14.95.   **(6)** This yard cart from Brookstone holds up to 160 pounds of cargo (including 24-inch firewood), yet it takes up little garage space because it folds to 42 by 29 by 10 inches. $62.95. Optional lawn tractor tow bar is $22.95.   **(7)** We all know about stacking baskets for magazines, papers, and toys, but don't overlook them for hobby materials. These are from Rubbermaid. $5 each.   **(8)** The Lervad 610 is Leichtung's solution for woodworkers who live in small spaces. It can be folded away (then permanently affixed whenever space becomes available), but can be used for everything (except large pieces like a grandfather clock) that a standard one can. $395. **(9)** Two feet of space is all you need for this single-unit washer/dryer from Frigidaire, which handles 10 pounds of clothes. $880.

10

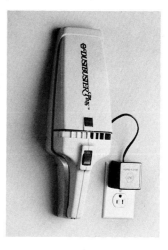

11

12

13

14

15

(10) Beautiful enough for a living or dining room, the Katonah file/storage cabinet has four drawers for legal- and letter-size files, plus two touch-latch cabinets with adjustable shelves. Designed by Paul Mayen and available in 14 colors, five woods, and five burls, from Intrex. From $1,920.   **(11)** A cordless hand-held vacuum cleaner takes up little space and is a big help for everyday clean-up jobs. Dustbuster Plus by Black & Decker has upholstery brush and crevice tool, plugs in to recharge continuously when not in use. $40.   **(12)** Engineers, students, hobbyists, and designers can work at home with a portable draftsman's table that has two covered compartments for instruments and two snap-on angled legs. Horizontal ruler of anodized aluminum stays parallel; quadrant's two 7-inch arms with en-

graved scales can be adjusted and locked; drawing surface is smooth white matte-finish plastic; 24$\frac{1}{2}$ by 19 inches, from Brookstone. $100.   **(13)** Wall-mounted bins swing out 180 degrees to reveal small workshop items, craft supplies, paper clips, and so on. Molded of white polystyrene, they have dividers to make small compartments. From Brookstone. $15.25.   **(14)** Fifty feet of flat hose winds up in one-eighth the space of conventional hose; case is 14$\frac{3}{8}$ by 9$\frac{5}{8}$ inches and 1 inch deep. Hose & Reel by Black & Decker. $25.   **(15)** Make your own foldaway worktable (or picnic table) with legs that screw into any tabletop 30 inches or more wide and 6 to 8 feet long. Legs are black steel tubing, 26 inches wide and 29 inches high. Brookstone. $37.95.   **(16)** The Palaset system, designed over 10 years ago, is a simple

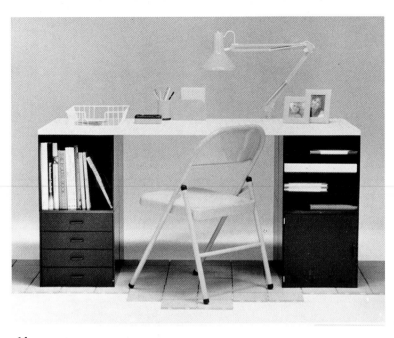

16

17

18

19

and extraordinarily useful system based on a 13½-inch cube that is available open, with shelves (up to three in a cube), with four drawers, or with a door and one shelf. Add a top to make a desk, stack them for children's toys, put four together for a low coffee table. In black or white; available at Conran's. Cubes start at $29.   **(17)** Sico's Ironing Center fits into the space between studs and features a fold-out board that swivels up to 180 degrees; electrical controls include iron plug-in, work light, and 30-minute shut-off timer. Recessed cabinet with solid oak frame has oak-veneer door Deluxe model, $426. Another good source is Iron-A-Way whose built-in ironing-board cabinet (not shown) has a pad-covered board with adjustable height; optional sleeveboard; an electric control panel with automatic

timer, appliance outlet, and work light; and a door that can be painted or papered to match the room. $289. **(18)** Black & Decker calls this hand truck a Haul In One. Use it to move garbage cans or air conditioners, then fold it up and hang it away when you're done. $60.   **(19)** Garrett Wade's small professional-style workbench in African mahogany measures only 53 inches long and 15½ inches wide and possesses all the features of full-size workbenches. Bench-dog system allows use with either tail or shoulder vises and permits clamping of workpieces up to 45 inches long. Deluxe version shown, $325; standard (without drawers), $225.

(1) Cookware that stacks is a real help in any kitchen, especially when it's needed for an "extra" appliance such as a microwave oven. Rubbermaid has developed this eight-piece microwave cookware set that nests into a compact 9 by 10½ by 6½ inches and gives you three casseroles, meat and vegetable cooker/steamer, roasting rack, cooking lid, and storage lids, in unbreakable white Micrel™ with clear covers. $44.95. **(2)** With its slim profile, Salton's Convection Toaster slips into small spaces on counters. $40. **(3)** A new addition to the Sears general catalog is this 3 in 1 Kitchen: cooking elements/sink/refrigerator in a 30-inch-wide steel cabinet. Sink and countertop are satin-finish stainless steel; refrigerator includes frozen food quick-use storage section; available in gas, 115 volt and 230 volt electric. $609.99. **(4)** In just 30 inches of space, this Cook-'N-Clean Center from Modern Maid combines an oven, cooktop (gas or electric), and full-size dishwasher that holds 16 place settings. The self-cleaning oven can broil with the door closed, and the dishwasher has an energy-saver setting. $1,625 to $1,700. **(5)** Store pots and pans on the wall with one of Taylor & Ng's Track Rack Systems, which can accommodate a shelf on top. About $47 in wood, $54 in wood and steel. **(6)** Here's a solid butcher-block worktable that doesn't take up a lot of space. The surface mea-

5

6

9

10

7

8

sures 24 inches wide by 25 inches deep, but it folds down to only 9½ inches. The backsplash doubles as a knife holder. From Brookstone. $220. **(7)** Sub-Zero refrigerators are favorites with decorators because they're 24 inches deep so they fit flush with base cabinets, and they accept front and side panels so they can be matched to any decor. A side-by-side that is 48 inches wide with an 18.7-cubic-foot refrigerator and 11.8-cubic-foot freezer is about $2,700. The company also makes under-counter units that fit nicely in island counters or can be used in dens. **(8)** Small enough to fit under a counter or be used at bedside, this two-door refrigerator is 33½ inches high, 18⅝ inches wide,

and 20¾ inches deep. It has door-panel inserts for five different looks, or you can use your own custom inserts. $329.99 at Sears stores, $319.99 through the Sears catalog. **(9)** If shelf space is limited, the Krups Cafethek is an ideal coffee/tea maker because it mounts on the wall. Features include a resting platform that can be raised or lowered for different-size receptacles, and a 24-hour digital clock with programming console. $190. **(10)** Adding an island such as this one from Taylor Woodcraft will provide work space, storage (this has drawers and cabinets front and rear), and an informal dining spot. $895. Optional pot rack holds spices, cookware, and lids. $165.

11

12

13

15

16

14

(11) Most standard refrigerators measure 30 inches wide, but this model from General Electric is only 28 inches with the same interior capacity as its 30-inch predecessor. The refrigerator has 15 cubic feet of total storage capacity; the freezer, 4.58 cubic feet. Door hinges and stops are reversible, so it can open in either direction. About $550.   **(12)** A vinyl-coated rack, attached to the underside of a shelf, holds glassware safely and, in deep shelves, allows space for plates below. From Lillian Vernon. About $6.   **(13)** An under-the-shelf basket puts frequently wasted space to good use. This one is from Heller. Three sizes; from $2.75 for the 12-inch.   **(14)** Stacking Slide-Out Drawers from Rubbermaid organize kitchen cabinets, make even small items easy to find. Drawers, $10 and $12; stacking kit, $3.50.   **(15)** An electric oven with timer and built-in counter light, two gas or electric burners, a sink, and a refrigerator with freezer compartment are all packed into this 30-inch-wide King Mini-Kitchen, available in five finishes. $1,180.   **(16)** You don't have to have a big kitchen to use a professional range. This unit from Wolf is only 23 inches wide and has four burners and an 18-inch-wide oven. Available in a baked-enamel or stainless-steel finish. As shown, $1,176 or $1,596.   **(17)** One

17

18

19

20

of the best sources for good-looking compact kitchens is Dwyer, whose complete units range from 39 to 96 inches wide and have many options, including microwave, dishwasher, and ice maker. This Series 51 model (51 inches wide) includes three electric burners, deep-bowl sink, oven/broiler, and 6-cubic-foot refrigerator. $1,910. **(18)** This slicer from Krups has a powerful motor and a slicer that adjusts from paper-thin to ³/₄-inch thickness—and folds up to only 3³/₄ inches, so it's easy to store. The food-collection tray folds into the machine. Three models, $65 to $95. **(19)** Because they have surface ventilation systems, eliminating the need

for outside venting or an overhead hood, Jenn-Air ranges can be installed anywhere in the kitchen. Interchangeable optional cooking elements (electric burners, ceramic cooktops, char-flavor grille, griddle, french-fry cooker, rotisserie attachments) put many functions into a small space. Available as a complete range or as a cooktop with two or three convertible elements. $450 and up. **(20)** This dishwasher from Admiral needs only 18 inches of width under the counter and is equipped with six cycle combinations, from plate warmer to pot and pan scrubber, plus an energy-saver option. $360.

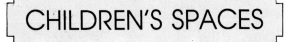

(1) Syroco's Fold Down Table measures 16 by 24 inches and would be handy for snacks or as a desk; since it supports up to 40 pounds, it can hold a typewriter. In five colors of heavy-duty thermoplastic. $25. **(2)** The Toobline system by H.U.D.D.L.E. gives children a multi-functional environment put together from optional components. This corner-bunk grouping includes two twin beds, a desk with drawer, a shelf with built-in study light, a bulletin board, and two full guard rails on the top bunk, which has a built-in ladder; a similar arrangement has the loft bed with a desk and bureau below. Both versions come in natural wood with yellow, green, or white vinyl "toobs." As shown, $1,095. **(3)** Part of a system of preschool and nursery furniture, this stackable injection-molded polyurethane chair would be a hard-wearing addition to a child's room. It comes in red, yellow, and signal blue and is $12^5/_8$ inches by $11^7/_8$ inches by $20^1/_2$ inches high. From Beylerian. $80. **(4)** This red-and-white bed from Muurame is a perfect first bed for a child who has just moved out of a crib and doesn't need much space. It measures $29^1/_2$ inches wide by only 54 inches long. When the child gets bigger, you can extend one end of the frame and drop in another section of mattress for a bed that's 87 inches long. With

4

5

6

7

optional storage drawer underneath (nice for extra blankets as well as toys), it's $350 from The Children's Room. **(5)** The Childspace crib by H.U.D.D.L.E. has a drawer underneath and a bureau with changing table on top; when the child is older, the crib converts to a youth bed. In white with bright color, $395, or pine, $445. Other systems from the firm have baby beds that convert to twin-size ones. **(6)** Finland's Muurame makes a broad range of children's beds and storage pieces that are terrific space-stretchers, some because of their well-designed flexibility and some because of their scaled-down sizes. This crib, for instance, measures

46 inches long by 24³/₄ inches wide by 35³/₄ inches high. The changing table can be removed and used with a cushion on top as an ottoman. At Scandinavian Design. Crib, $328 with mattress; changing table, $129. **(7)** In the space of a single bed, this Childspace Chestbed by H.U.D.D.L.E. gives a child a bed, four drawers, a trundle for a friend, and a place for clip-in shelves; in white with a choice of bright colors, $365, or pine, $415. Like other systems from this firm, it is shipped KD (knocked down) and can be assembled with a screwdriver.

8

9

10

11

(8) Any small child would enjoy this pine table (28 inches wide by 24 inches deep by 24½ inches high) and two chairs. It's nice for games when the chairs (seats are 13 inches high) are opposite; or the top can be raised to an angle to use it for drawing (inside it's a storage box). When not in use, the two chairs fit snugly against the frame side by side. From the Children's Room. $189.   **(9)** This loft bed has space under it that can be used as a play area by small children; young teenagers might like to put pillows and a record player there. Other options in this Jungmanni system from Muurame allows you to add another bed plus trundle at floor level so that three can sleep in the floor space of a single bed. More pieces include desks, bookshelves of varying dimensions, and wardrobe closets.

Bed only as shown, $596 including mattress and two guard rails. From Scandinavian Design.   **(10,11)** There are more than 500 possible combinations from the pieces in the Bunk Trunk Collection from Room Plus Furniture. The "body" of the pieces comes in white, beige, and butcher-block mica finishes; the drawer and cabinet fronts in 20 finishes, including bright colors. One popular configuration is the loft bed, which takes up only 6 feet 6 inches of space in length, even when it incorporates such pieces as drawers and desk on its two ends. One of its advantages is that it can be used as a loft bed with storage underneath for a few years and then, if desired, be broken down to a bed and a wall system. The teen boy's version shown here would be about $2,600; the young girl's, about $1,400.

DIRECTORY OF MANUFACTURERS

Admiral (M)/Division of Magic Chef
1701 East Woodfield Road
Schaumburg, Illinois 60196
(312) 884-2600

American-Standard (M)
P.O. Box 2003
New Brunswick, New Jersey 08903
(800) 821-7700, ext. 4023

Arise Futon Mattress Co., Inc. (R)
37 Wooster Street
New York, New York 10013
(212) 925-0310

Atelier International, Ltd. (T)
595 Madison Avenue
New York, New York 10022
(212) 644-0400

Beylerian Limited (T)
305 East 63rd Street
New York, New York 10021
(212) 755-6303

Black & Decker (U.S.), Inc. (M)
515 Glebe Road
Easton, Maryland 21601
(301) 822-6770

Brookstone Company (MO)
127 Vose Farm Road
Peterborough, New Hampshire 03458
(603) 924-7181

Casa Bella Imports (T)
979 Third Avenue
New York, New York 10022
(212) 688-2020

Castro Convertibles Corp. (M, R)
1990 Jericho Turnpike
New Hyde Park, New York 11040
(516) 488-3000

The Children's Room, Inc. (R)
318 East 45th Street
New York, New York 10017
(212) 687-3868

Clairson International (M)
720 S.W. 17th Street
Ocala, Florida 32670
(904) 732-8734

Conran's (R, MO)
145 Huguenot Street (MO)
New Rochelle, New York 10801
(914) 632-0515; (800) 431-2718

Curtis Co., Inc. (R)
31 East 31st Street
New York, New York 10016
(212) 689-1616

Design Institute America, Inc. (T, M)
123 Empire Street
Montpelier, Ohio 43543
(419) 485-5551

Design Selections International, Inc. (T)
150 East 58th Street
New York, New York 10155
(212) 751-1321

Devin Company, Inc. (T)
4801 Exposition Boulevard
Los Angeles, California 90016
(213) 731-4181

Dux (T)
305 East 63rd Street
New York, New York 10021
(212) 752-3897

Dwyer Products Corp. (M)
Calumet Avenue
Michigan City, Indiana 46360
(219) 874-5236

Elfa Space Saver System
distributed by Scan-Plast, Inc. (M)
54 East 54th Street
New York, New York 10022
(212) 755-0422

Eljer Plumbingware (M)
1201 Corbin Street
Port Elizabeth, New Jersey 07201
(201) 527-1800

Excel Wood Products Co., Inc. (M)
One Excel Plaza
Lakewood, New Jersey 08701
(201) 364-2000

Frigidaire (M)
1 Woodbridge Center, Suite 210
Woodbridge, New Jersey 07095
(201) 636-2300

Garrett Wade Co., Inc. (R, MO)
161 Avenue of the Americas
New York, New York 10013
(212) 807-1155

General Electric (M)
(800) 626-2000

Hansen Lamps (T)
121 East 24th Street
New York, New York 10010
(212) 674-2130

Hastings Tile & Il Bagno Collections
201 East 57th Street (T)
New York, New York 10022
(212) 755-2710 and
404 Northern Boulevard (R)
Great Neck, New York 11021
(516) 482-1840

Heller Designs, Inc. (M)
41 Madison Avenue
New York, New York 10010
(212) 685-4200

Hickory Chair Company (M)
P.O. Box 2147
Hickory, North Carolina 28603
(704) 328-1801

H.U.D.D.L.E. (R, MO)
3416 Wesley Street
Culver City, CA 90230
(213) 836-8001

ICF, Inc. (T)
305 East 63rd Street
New York, New York, 10021
(212) 750-0900

**Intrex, Inc. (T),
a subsidiary of Habitat
International, Ltd.**
150 East 58th Street
New York, New York 10155
(212) 758-0926

Iron-a-Way, Inc. (M)
220 West Jackson Street
Morton, Illinois 61550
(309) 266-7232

Italyca, Inc. (T, R)
215 Lexington Avenue
New York, New York 10016
(212) 684-1199

Jenn-Air Corporation (M)
3035 Shadeland Avenue
Indianapolis, Indiana 46226
(317) 545-2271

Kalwall Corp. (M)
1111 Candia Road
Manchester, New Hamsire 03103
(603) 627-3861

King Refrigerator Corporation (M)
76-02 Woodhaven Boulevard
Glendale, New York 11385
(212) 897-2200

The Kittinger Company (T)
305 East 63rd Street
New York, New York 10021
(212) 398-8660

Kloss Video Corp. (M)
145 Sidney Street
Cambridge, Massachusetts 02139
(617) 547-6363

Kohler Co. (M)
Kohler, Wisconsin 53044
(414) 457-4441

Robert Krups North America (M)
7 Pearl Court
Allendale, New Jersey 07401
(201) 825-1116

The Lane Co., Inc. (M)
Altavista, Virginia 24517
(804) 369-5641

Lasco (M)
Anaheim, California 92806
(714) 993-1220

Leichtung, Inc. (MO)
4944 Commerce Parkway
Cleveland, Ohio 44128
(216) 831-6191

Lillian Vernon (MO)
510 South Fulton Avenue
Mount Vernon, New York 10550
(914) 699-4131

Mitsubishi Electric Sales America (M)
3030 East Victoria Street
Rancho Dominguez, California 90221
(213) 537-7132

Modern Maid Co. (M), a Raytheon Company
403 North Main Street
Topton, Pennsylvania 19562
(215) 682-4211

Murphy Door Bed Co., Inc. (M)
40 East 34th Street
New York, New York 10016
(212) 682-8936

Panasonic Company (M)
1 Panasonic Way
Secaucus, New Jersey 07094
(201) 348-7000

Pioneer Video, Inc. (M)
200 West Grand Avenue
Montvale, New Jersey 07645
(201) 573-1122

Plaza Towel Holder Co., Inc. (M)
2016 North Broadway
Wichita, Kansas 67214
(316) 267-4233

Rakks System/Rangine Corp. (M)
144 Moody Street
Waltham, Massachusetts 02154
(617) 899-1600

Room Plus Furniture (R)
stores in New York City, Long Island,
Westchester, and New Jersey
1555 Third Avenue
New York, New York 10028
(212) 410-9393

Rubbermaid Incorporated (M)
Wooster, Ohio 44691
(216) 264-6464

Salton, Inc. (M)
1260 Zerega Avenue
Bronx, New York 10462
(212) 931-3900

Scandinavian Design, Inc. (T, R)
127 East 59th Street
New York, New York 10022
(212) 755-6078

Sears, Roebuck and Co. (R, MO)
800 stores nationwide, plus catalog

Sharp Electronics Corporation (M)
10 Sharp Plaza
Paramus, New Jersey 07652
(201) 265-5600

Sherwood Corp. (M)
P.O. Box 519
Spring City, Tennessee 37381
(615) 365-5453

Sico, Inc. (M)
P.O. Box 1169
Minneapolis, Minnesota 55440
(612) 941-1700

Sony Consumer Products Company (M)
Sony Drive
Park Ridge, New Jersey 07656
(800) 222-SONY

Steelcase, Inc. (M)
299 Park Avenue
New York, New York 10171
(212) 421-5060

Sub-Zero Freezer Co., Inc. (M)
P.O. Box 4130
Madison, Wisconsin 53711
(608) 271-2233

Sunar (T)
730 Fifth Avenue
New York, New York 10019
(212) 246-5200

Syroco Housewares (M)
P.O. Box 4875
Syracuse, New York 13221
(315) 635-9911

Taylor & Ng (M)
P.O. Box 200
Brisbane, California 94005
(415) 467-2600

Taylor Woodcraft, Inc. (M)
P.O. Box 245
South River Road
Malta, Ohio 43758
(614) 962-3741

Thayer Coggin, Inc. (M)
P.O. Box 5867
427 South Road
High Point, North Carolina 27262
(919) 883-0111

White-Westinghouse Appliance Company (M)
930 Fort Duquesne Boulevard
Pittsburgh, Pennsylvania 15222
(412) 263-3700

Wolf Range Co. (M)
19600 South Alameda Street
Compton, California 90224
(213) 637-3737

Workbench, Inc. (R)
470 Park Avenue South (main store)
New York, New York 10016
(212) 532-7900

Barry Berkus
Berkus Group Architects
1531 Chapala Street
Santa Barbara, California 93101
(805) 963-8901

Eric Bernard Unlimited, Inc.
177 East 94th Street
New York, New York 10028
(212) 876-9295

Bruce Bierman Design
29 West 15th Street
New York, New York 10011
(212) 243-1935

Geri Blair Interiors
381 Main Street
New Canaan, Connecticut 06840
(203) 966-2822

Laura Bohn and **Joseph Lembo**
Lembo/ Bohn Design Associates
116 West 29th Street
New York, New York 10001
(212) 947-0547

Mario Buatta, Incorporated
120 East 80th Street
New York, New York 10021
(212) 988-6811

Alan Buchsbaum Design Coalition
12 Greene Street
New York, New York 10013
(212) 966-3010

Bump Zoid
260 Fifth Avenue
New York, New York 10001
(212) 684-7471

Leonard Colchamiro PC, AIA
Architects and Planners
133 Berkeley Place
Brooklyn, New York 11217
(212) 638-5442

Lorraine Cook Interiors
61 Irving Place
New York, New York 10003
(212) 228-8609

Gary Crain Interiors
211 East 70th Street
New York, New York 10021
(212) 734-7847

Francis Dearden
Decorative designer and painter
Long Island, New York
(516) 367-4332

Ruben de Saavedra Ltd.
225 East 57th Street
New York, New York 10022
(212) 759-2892

Dexter Design, Inc.
133 East 58th Street
New York, New York 10022
(212) 752-2426

T. Keller Donovan, Inc.
230 Central Park South
New York, New York 10019
(212) 245-2391

Melvin Dwork, Inc.
405 East 56th Street
New York, New York 10022
(212) 759-9330

Beverly Ellsley Interiors
87 Redcoat Road
Westport, Connecticut 06880
(203) 227-1157

Mark Epstein Designs, Inc.
340 East 66th Street
New York, New York 10021
(212) 734-1792

Horace Gifford
310 East 46th Street
New York, New York 10017
(212) 490-1527

Mariette Himes Gomez Associates
241 East 78th Street
New York, New York 10021
(212) 288-6856

Joan Halperin Interior Design
401 East 80th Street
New York, New York 10021
(212) 288-8636

Michael Haskins
435 Park Avenue South
New York, New York 10016
(212) 696-0552

Carl Hribar Architect
106 East 19th Street
New York, New York 10003
(212) 674-8135

Keith Irvine and Thomas Fleming, Inc.
19 East 57th Street
New York, New York 10022
(212) 888-6000

Marc Klein Interiors, Ltd.
30 Sycamore Lane
Roslyn Heights, New York 11577
(516) 484-1682

Ann LeConey
755 Park Avenue
New York, New York 10022
(212) 472-1265

Lemeau & Llana
325 Bleecker Street
New York, New York 10014
(212) 675-5190

Sybil Levin Interiors
339 East 57th Street
New York, New York 10022
(212) 888-0920

Robert K. Lewis Associates, Inc.
300 East 59th Street
New York, New York 10022
(212) 755-1557

Richard Mervis Design, Inc.
790 Madison Avenue
New York, New York, 10021
(212) 737-6363

John Robert Moore II
Interior Design
41 East 68th Street
New York, New York 10021
(212) 249-9370

Charles Morris Mount, Inc.
200 West 72nd Street
New York, New York 10023
(212) 799-6360

Richard Lowell Neas
157 East 71st Street
New York, New York 10021
(212) 772-1878

Tom O'Toole, Inc.
145 East 92nd Street
New York, New York 10028
(212) 348-0639

Patino/Wolf Associates, Inc.
400 East 52nd Street
New York, New York 10022
(212) 355-6581

Shattuck/Blair Associates
312 West 78th Street
New York, New York 10024
(212) 496-7545

Shope Reno Wharton Associates
18 West Putnam Avenue
Greenwich, Connecticut 06830
(203) 869-7250

Marshall-Schule Associates, Inc.
220 East 73rd Street
New York, New York 10021
(212) 772-7441

Kevin Walz
Walz Design
141 Fifth Avenue
New York, New York 10010
(212) 477-2211

Zajac & Callahan, Incorporated
304 East 49th Street
New York, New York 10017
(212) 832-8690

INDEX